Eken Press & Grenadine Publishing
6 Artichoke Mews
Artichoke Place
London se 5 8ts
United Kingdom
www.grenadine.se

CAVA – Spain's Premium Sparkling Wine
© Grenadine Publishing and Anna Wallner 2018

First Edition
ISBN 978-1-908233-12-7

Photo:
Andréas Wallner: 2, 3, 8, 14, 22, 23, 25, 26, 30, 32.2, 37, 40, 41.2, 42.2, 43, 44, 45, 51, 55, 57, 61, 64, 65, 78, 80, 81, 82, 84, 85, 86, 88, 89, 90, 92.1, 92.2, 92.4-9, 110, 111.
Anna Wallner: 36.1, 38, 39, 62, 108.
Blai Carda: 36.2, 41.1, 48, 49.
Malin Jernkrook: 106, backside of book.
Frida Johansson Metso: 11, 12, 16, 18, 19, 52, 54, 58, 60, 65, 66.
Codorníu: 20, 23, 42.1, 47, 92.3.
Institut del Cava: 33.2.
Consejo Regulador del Cava: 28, 31, 32.1, 33.1, 34, 35, 56.
Ulrika Ekblom (*photographer*)/Liselotte Forslin (*stylist*): 69, 71, 72, 75, 77.
Cover picture: iStockphoto.com

Graphic design and production: Alan Maranik

Printed by: Print Best, Estonia 2018

Reach Anna at:
Web: www.annawallner.se
Facebook: www.facebook.com/thecavalady
Twitter: @thecavalady

Anna Wallner

CAVA

Spain's premium sparkling wine

GRENADINE

EKEN
PRESS

For my husband Andréas and my children,
who are my moon and stars.

May God keep you, O Catalan vine!
A green sea which stretches out to the mountains!
My breast swells when I breathe in your glory
if my feet are buried in your leaves!
As your shoots embrace the earth,
may our people embrace above.
O vine of the plain and the mountain,
give us strength and nobility forever!

Àngel Guimerà

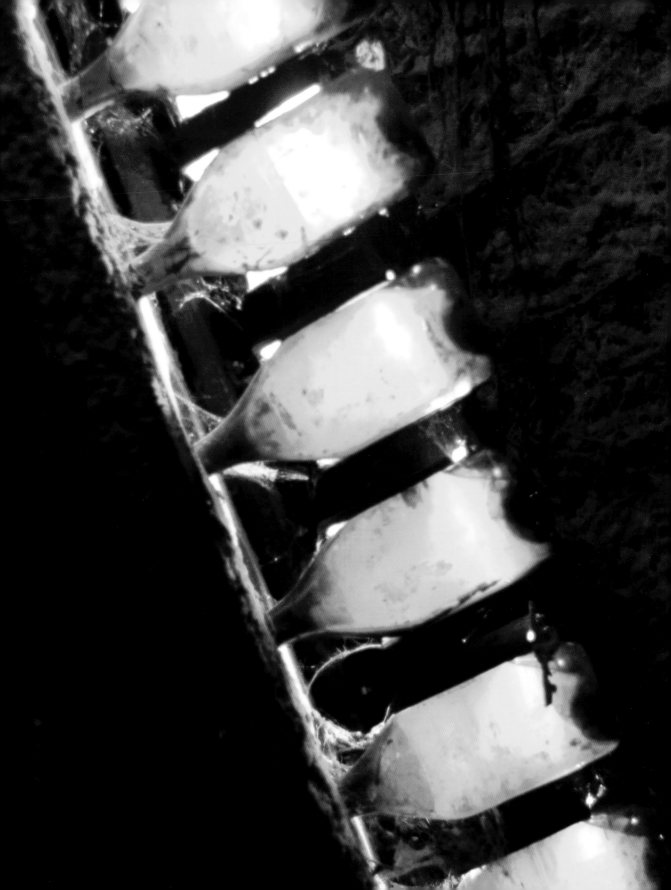

TABLE OF CONTENTS

BUBBLES MAKE YOU HAPPY!

There is something special about bubbles. With a glass of sparkling wine in your hand, life just becomes easier in some way. Whether if it's Champagne, Cava, Prosecco or Sekt is perhaps less important, because the bubbles themselves have an exuberant effect on mood and life.

I grew up in a family where Champagne was served on New Year's Eve only, never seeing other types of sparkling during my childhood. It was only when I met my husband that I realized the pure magic of sparkling wine. He loved both Cava and Champagne, and happily served me these bubbles with all kinds of foods—which I had never experienced before. Nowadays, we open a bottle of bubbles whenever we get the chance—always having at least one bottle in the fridge. I highly recommend you adopt this habit too, because you never know when you might need it. And it also makes everyday life so much more fun.

I truly believe that we'd all be much happier if we could just learn to enjoy life on a bit more and rejoice in the good things around us.

Maybe you're like me… An extremely fortunate person, who has friends, family, all the love and a comfortable home. In other words, things to be extremely thankful for—things to celebrate.

Most people seldomly celebrate, rather just rushing on with their everyday lives—forgetting what's really important. But I believe it's the small things that matter, so why not take the chance to remember them? Open a bottle of bubbles, sit down and take in the moment. The reason can be anything, really. Maybe you just got a new job, bought a dog, finished the renovation of your house or just survived your child's fifth birthday party.

So be sure to keep a bottle of bubbles in your fridge always, because you never know when it will come in handy.

I hope you enjoy this book and that it helps you discover the special sensation of sparkling wine. My greatest joy would be that if this book helps you celebrate at least one of your life's little moments more, then my work will have been worth it!

Salud and cheers!

THE JOURNEY CONTINUES

My mother always says that "things happen for a reason". Maybe you can't see it, because you're in the middle of it all—but in time, you will. I'm starting to see it now, what all the work was for and how it's changed me. Not only myself —my family, my friends and people around me have experienced the change too.

Through my work with Cava, I have gained so much experience, knowledge, friends and in truth a new life. Our plans for the future has been altered, and our children will forever be affected by the change in my career. They will find it normal to have winemakers as "aunties" and "uncles"; that Swedish, Spanish, Catalan and English are spoken in a constant mix around them. They will know the differences between vines as any other Swede would know the difference between trees in the forest. It's fantastic to think about the power behind our choices, and I'm excited about what the future might bring. One thing I know now is that I will never let Penedès go, and I will continue to help spread the passion, love and happiness these bubbles and their creators have given to me.

Why Cava?

It all started during my studies to become sommelier. I became increasingly interested in sparkling wine. I bought every book on the subject I could lay my hands on, which resulted in a solid library of Champagne literature.

My frustration not finding any literature on the other sparkling wines grew. And when I discovered that three-quarters of the "Encyclopedia of Sparkling Wines" consisted of texts on Champagne, that was the straw that broke the camel's back. What about Italian Prosecco, German Sekt, South African Cap Classique, Australian sparkling wine or Russian champanskij? Where was the Spanish Cava? Cava is after all, the most-exported bubbles in the world, but you'll only find at most—a single page on the subject in wine literature.

After much searching, I finally found one book dedicated to Cava. I'll say that again: Just. One. So I decided to do something about it.

What you hold in your hand is the second edition of the book dedicated to Cava, its creators, the land it comes from and everyone who loves these bubbles.

Anna Wallner
Uppsala January 2018

LOVED AND MORE POPULAR THAN EVER

Cava is the world's most-exported sparkling wine in terms of bottles. In 1980, a total of 28 million bottles of Cava were produced and 12 percent of these were exported. In 2016, the production had increased to 245 million bottles, of which 65 percent were sold outside Spain. These figures show how massively Cava has grown and also how much is consumed by us living outside Spain.

Although Cava's popularity has grown immensely, too many of us still drink these Spanish bubbles more or less completely without thought. Unlike Champagne, it seems that many people drink Cava without knowing much about the product itself, its history, geography, production, grapes or anything that makes this sparkling wine so special. Most of the consumers I have met would in earlier years have chosen Cava when they wanted an inexpensive fizz.

In recent days, Cava is finally starting to get the attention it deserves. People are slowly learning that Cava and Champagne should not be compared, and that they have different characteristics—used for different occasions and each enjoyed for their own qualities.

Before this trend started, we were lucky if we found the good Cavas outside Spain. And even if we did find them, most of us were unaware of our luck. Since they nudged the same price range as the cheapest Champagnes, and due to our history and upbringing we chose the Champagne, against better judgement, just because the name on the label was Champagne.

How can this be? Frankly, because we—as consumers—have been more interested in what it says on the bottle, than in the contents of the bottle itself.

Many of us know nothing about Cava. How could we have learned? There's no literature or information. We have wallowed in our ignorance, thinking that Cava is a cheap Spanish fizz. We could not be more mistaken! When it comes to Champagne, the situation is reversed. Here we have been able to read book after book on the subject to our hearts content. Even if we weren't interested, we couldn't escape the fact that *"Champagne should be cold, dry and free of charge"*, as Churchill once said.

And if we have had that interest, there are many other references showing the influence of

Champagne on our history. And sure, Cava has been around for a long time, but it's actually recently that we have begun to open our eyes to this amazing sparkling wine.

Technology advances and innovations, research and passionate commitments make today's Cava better than ever, and the world has noticed. These producers are experts in sparkling wine and have fresh ideas, passion and enthusiasm as their key drivers. But honestly, they are just following the tradition and background that has been passed on to them for generations.

Did you know that ...
From 1980 to 2010 there has been an increase from 82 Cava producers to 256.

HOW CAVA CAME TO BE

Spain has produced wines far longer than they have produced sparkling wines. But exactly when the vine was introduced to the Iberian Peninsula is a bit unclear and, to some extent, a matter of some controversy. Some historians believe that it was the Phoenicians who brought the plants, when they traded throughout the Mediterranean. Others believe that it was the Greeks who were the first to introduce vines, with their colonization of the land between 700 and 600 BC. However, it is certain that the vine was well known and formed a large part of the agriculture by 300 BC, when the Romans conquered the Iberian Peninsula.

During the time of the Empire wine and oil became the two main goods exported from the Spanish provinces to Rome. The cultivated areas where vines were grown expanded over time and spread inland from the coast as the planting of grapevines and wine production became increasingly common. When the Moors occupied parts of what is present-day Spain in the 700s, the vines were largely uprooted and wine production thereby suffered. The Islamic faithful Moors, as the Muslims today, did not have alcohol on their menu.

Reborn like the Phoenix, the vineyards were resurrected by the Christian monks who started to build their monasteries, where the Moors retreated. The monks loved wine as much as the Moors disliked it. This is understandable since the wine is a very important part of the Holy Communion. This meant that new vineyards were planted wherever new monasteries were founded. Where there was a monastery, there was also a vineyard, and soon, the common people took vine cultivation into their own hands. The monasteries came to serve as centers of wine knowledge. The Franciscan monk Francesc Eiximenius (1349-1409) left many texts behind, which address all aspects related to wine and its production. In these texts, he refers to "tingling" wines, which could be interpreted as slightly sparkling, and "jumping" wines, which could refer to the lids of amphorae—insisting they jump off due to the increasing internal pressure.

During 16th and 17th centuries, viticulture flourished during the Renaissance period in France, while Catalonia and many parts of Spain suffered from political and economic problems, and labour shortages. The winds changed at the end of the 17th century when European trade increased, largely thanks to the trade with the American colonies. Catalonia was able to exploit this new situation and got

The town of Sant Sadurní

back on its feet—becoming the center for the enormous expansion that occurred during the 18th century.

Spanish wine production got another lucky push in 1778, when King Carlos III approved free trade in the American colonies, which made the wine industry enormously lucrative.

The story of Cava, as we know it today, started about 100 years after King Carlos' decree. Although there had been sparkling wines made in Spain earlier, it was really in the early 19th century that the traditional method started to be used and bear fruit. In the town of Sant Sadurní d'Anoia, focus was placed on mastering the traditional method and, little by little, the results got better. By the end of the century, the sparkling wines won international competitions at the world fairs in both Vienna in 1873, and Paris in 1889. And in 1872, Josef Raventós uncorked the first bottle—made from the grapes Macabeu, Xarel-lo and Parellada, coming to be the three signature grapes of Cava.

However, just a few years later winemakers in Sant Sadurní d'Anoia would have to change their focus to something much less pleasant: The wine louse.

The wine louse, *Phylloxera vastatrix*, came to Europe from California in 1863 and spread through the French vineyards—sucking the sap from vine roots. By 1879 Phylloxera had crossed the mountain range and gained a foothold in Costa Brava, south of the French border. Come 1883, the louse reached Sant Sadurní

d'Anoia in its conquest of the Iberian Peninsula and nine years later, 90 percent of the vineyards in the area had been affected. The only cure proved to be grafting the European vine *Vitis Vinifera* onto the American vine *Vitis Rupestris*, whose roots had proved to be immune to the Phylloxera attacks. While the required replanting of the vineyards took place, many vintners took the opportunity to optimize and restructure their vineyards to better suit the sparkling wine production.

With the Phylloxera defeated and their improved vineyards, the future seemed to be bright for the wine producers. One advancement was the art contest in 1898, arranged by Manuel Raventós and his house Codorníu. Here, internationally renowned artists such as Utrillo, Casas, Tubilla and Junyent contributed works of art, all with cava themes, that have since become classics. Also, King Alfonso III's visit to the Penedés in 1904, strengthened the region's position as producers of high quality sparkling wines and in 1911 the sales of domestic sparkling wine outnumbered imported versions, such as Champagne.

During the early 1900s, development continued strongly—despite the ravages of the First World War. Thanks to the producers' never-ending commitment, Cava began to spread seriously beyond Spain's borders, and in 1935, the house of Freixenet had expanded their exports to America. Going forward, neither the Spanish Civil War nor World War II were positive events when it came to development or growth, but they only had the effect of holding back the expanding production.

From the time the producers began to export their bubbles until the mid-1900s, the sparkling wine from Catalonia was usually referred to as Xampany, Champaña or Spanish Champagne. The last name was largely due to the extensive exports to England. In the mid-1950s, Spanish Champagne had become so popular and widely known that the French Champagne farmers began to get irritated. "Champagne is Champagne" they thought, and took some of the Spanish companies to court. In 1960 after appeals from the French, came so the final verdict in the matter, which ruled that the name Champagne could only be used for sparkling wine from the Champagne region in France. The producers in Spain did not take this too hard, since they had already started to use the word Cava a few years earlier for their sparkling wines, even in official texts and documents. But it was not until the Spanish entry into the EU in 1986, that the status of the term "Cava" would be reserved for quality sparkling wines produced using the traditional method, in a determined region, and in accordance with the regulations and rules set down by the Consejo Regulador del Cava, which is the supervisory board for Cava. To distinguish the different sparkling wines from one another, a mark with different geometric shapes was adopted on the bottom of the corks.

An equilateral triangle applied to wines that got their bubbles through the addition of carbon dioxide, as used for soft drinks.

A rectangle is for the wines that are fermented in the bottle for a very limited time, then filtered to remove the sediments and rebottled.

A circle is for the wines that have undergone their second fermentation in pressure tanks, and are then bottled.

And the four-pointed star is saved for the quality wines that have undergone the time consuming and labour intensive traditional method.

From then on, the four-pointed star has become Cava's hallmark—always visible on the bottom of the cork.

Since Cava acquired its name, the wine has spread worldwide and taken market after market by storm.

S.XII

S.XV

S.XIX

S.I

CAVA AND CHAMPAGNE: SIMILAR AND STARKLY DIFFERENT

I am awfully tired of people comparing Champagne and Cava. Most people don't compare all red wines with a classic Bordeaux, and those who might would most likely be seen as narrow-minded. But when it comes to sparkling wines people don't apply the same sense... Cava, prosecco, sekt etc. is not Champagne and nor are these wines trying to be, just as Champagne is not trying to be anything else than Champagne. These styles are unique in their own character and although, in the case of Cava and Champagne, the two wines are produced using the same traditional method, there is far more that distinguishes them from one another.

The product named Cava is, as mentioned previously, protected and controlled by the Consejo Regulador del Cava, which is in charge of current regulations and any amendments thereof. Here, everything is regulated, from the grapes that are allowed to be used for production of Cava, to the number of hectoliters of must that can be drawn from a hectare of land. They also keep records of all the producers and statistics on all productions, exports and sales. Consejo Regulador also makes detailed inspections during harvest time and carries out quality checks on all the producers' products before they go to domestic market or exported – ensuring that Cava is upholding high enough standards. Next time you buy a bottle of cava, you will see their little sticker seal of approval on top of the cork or on the bottle itself.

Geography

The areas that make up the DO (denominación de origen) Cava comprises of a total of 159 municipalities, all located within ten provinces; Barcelona, Tarragona, Lleida, Girona, La Rioja, Álava, Zaragoza, Navarra, Valencia and Badajoz. Although the DO is quite large, 95 percent of all Cava is produced within Catalonia, mainly in Penedès. The center of Penedès and Cava production has been the city of Sant Sadurní d'Anoia, located about 40 kilometres west of Barcelona.

To the North is the impressive mountain of Montserrat, a rock formation with both very special geological structure and appearance, and is of enormous spiritual relevance for many Christians. To the South, the border is formed

95 percent of all Cava is produced within Catalonia, mainly in Penedès

by the Mediterranean Sea, while in the East it takes the form of "el puente del diablo de Martorell", the devil bridge in Martorell, of which there is also told a famous legend. The border in the west is marked by another Roman monument, the triumphal arch in Berá. The valley is also protected in the West and East by mountains, however, neither as high nor as majestically beautiful as the Montserrat. All these surrounding mountains ensure a stable climate in Penedès and protect the valley from the cold winds coming in from the North. This is very beneficial when it comes to grape culturing since the grapes do not tolerate winds that are too cold. So, although the quality of the harvest yields naturally varies from year to year, it is largely thanks to the surrounding mountains that they are so high and of such a consistent quality in Penedès.

Climate and soil

Spain is known for its mild and sunny climate, and the Anoia valley is no exception. Thanks to the warm Mediterranean to the south and, as mentioned, the mountain of Montserrat as a protection against the cold north wind, the grapes here grow in a protected environment. With mild winters and warm summers the growing season is long. The grapes mature slowly—producing a high sugar content. The warmth comes early in the morning during the summer and lasts until the breeze comes. Blowing in from the Mediterranean Sea in the late afternoon; it gives some much needed freshness to the grapes. I never thought it was possible that a wind could be so punctual, but the producers told me that it has to do with the closeness to the sea. Certainly it rains too, but it is only heavy rains or hail close to harvest that constitute an actual threat. Thanks to these conditions, the harvests

THE LEGEND OF THE DEVIL BRIDGE IN MARTORELL

A long time ago in the small town of Martorell there was an innkeeper who had to walk to a well to fetch water. The well was situated on the other side of the river Llobregat and the only way to pass the river to reach the well on the other side was to jump on the stones in the ford. However, sometimes the river rose so much that the stones could not be seen and the innkeeper, could thus not pass the river, and was therefore without water until the river would fall back. One day, when the innkeeper found himself in desperate need of water, the river had risen and the stones were impossible to find. Standing searching on the riverbank, he became so angry that he cursed. Suddenly a fine gentleman appeared out of the fog on the riverbank. He came up to the innkeeper and said "This night, before the rooster crows at dawn, I can build a bridge, steady and strong, so that you can cross the river whenever it suits you... As a token of gratitude, I would expect, if I give you the bridge within the agreed time, that you give me your soul the day you leave this mortal life." The landlord was so angry that he did not think on the consequences and accepted the gentleman's proposal. He returned home and told his family about the strange incident and they all realized that it must have been the Devil himself that the innkeeper had met there on the riverbank. Despite his family's warnings they did not worry the landlord, for he thought he had reached a good agreement with the gentleman. But as the night progressed, the anger subsided with the man, and he began to think that it must have been the Devil after all, and that he had been caught in a trap. Assuming that was true, how could he break free from this agreement? The gentleman himself had said that the bridge would be completed before the rooster crowed, and if this somehow could be prevented and the bridge was unfinished the pact would be null and void. When the dreaded hour approached, the landlord rose out of bed and boiled a kettle of water. When the water was steaming hot, he took the kettle off the hook, went out into the yard and poured the water over the non-suspecting rooster, which in pain let out a loud COCK-A-DOODLE-DOO, despite the early hour. The innkeeper then rushed down to the river where he earlier met the gentleman. There, at the site stood a large and permanent bridge as promised but the rooster's early crowing meant that the last stone had not yet been put into place and so the bridge was not completely finished.

Visitors can even now see the place of the missing last stone and the bridge stands unfinished until this very day.

are very consistent, compared with many other wine regions around the world.

Cava grapes are grown everywhere in the hilly countryside of Penedès, and are planted at altitudes between 100-800 meters (about 300-2600 ft) above sea level. Some Cava producers have also recently begun to experiment with plantations at higher elevations. If the temperature can be kept down thanks to the high altitudes while still accessing the same amount of sunshine, they will get both the sought-after acid in the wine and the sugar that is needed to achieve the right strength of alcohol and fruit sweetness in the finished product.

The soil in the area is largely calcareous due to the fact that the valley once was a seabed. These chalky soils are considered a great advantage in the production of sparkling wine. The limestone in the soil gives the wines some of the minerality in their aroma and taste that many wine drinkers appreciate in sparkling wines. There are also other minerals in the ground, such as iron, magnesium and phosphorus. The composition of this reddish soil with its stones and calcium deposits provide the vineyards with a natural drainage to protect plants during heavy rainfalls.

During my visits to producers in the region, I have understood that it is customary to divide the area into three parts. Firstly, is the area closest to the sea that enjoys the slightly warmer Mediterranean climate. Secondly, the plain formed between the mountains which is situated a bit higher than the coastal area and is thus a little cooler. Thirdly, the hillsides on the surrounding mountains where the climate is even cooler,

thanks to the higher elevations. These three areas all have different microclimates that affect the final product. And with practice, great interest and searching among Cava producers, you may appreciate the differences between the types of soil in which the grapes have been grown.

When it comes to these three areas, you will find that there are certain grapes varieties grown in certain places by tradition. Different types of grape thrive in different kinds of soils and at different altitudes. It is therefore of high importance for the producers to optimize their plots. In order to make the best choice of variety when planting new vines, there is always a rigorous analysis of soil and everything else that makes the plant site unique. Soil type, altitude, sun exposure and drainage are just a few parameters that are taken into account. Nothing is left to chance.

In Penedès, there's a long tradition of ecological and sustainable farming. However, due to the fact that many producers are quite small, the heavy bureaucratic paperwork required to obtain the ecological seal of approval has stopped many from trying to get the certification. But I should point out that the number of ecological Cavas on the market grow every year, which is fantastic.

The thoughts about caring for the earth take many forms in the area. Some make their own composts, keep goats grazing the vineyards after harvest, keep bees for pollination or lean towards the bio-dynamic practices—like the houses of Recaredo, Gramona and Parés Baltà, to mention just a few. But all producers have their own ways to keep the land as immaculate as possible.

Macabeo

Xarel-lo

Grapes

The special character, and the fresh fruiti-ness that often characterizes Cava come from the nine grape varieties that are allowed. The most traditional blends are a mix of, Parellada, Xarel-lo and Macabeu, all green varieties. Also Malvasia and Chardonnay are green grapes that are allowed for the production. The blue varieties are Garnacha, Monastrell, Trepat and Pinot Noir.

Macabeu [məkə'βew]

Macabeu, sometimes also called Viura, is the first of the three traditional grapes that ripen in late summer and is usually harvested in early September or even August. It grows in large bunches, green and compact—giving high yields. With its thin skin it is a little more sensitive than most grapes when it comes to frosty nights and pest infestations. Despite this, Macabeu is relatively easy to grow as it thrives in most soil types and it also adapts well to dif-ferent climates and altitudes. The variety is of-ten described as elegant, with medium acidity and moderate alcohol, and can contribute a lot of fruitiness, like green apples and pears. It also often gives a nice balance to the final blends. Macabeu is at the moment the most cultivated grape for Cava, and is grown mainly in central Penedès and further out towards the coast.

Xarel-lo [ʃə'rɛɬ:u]

This grape was once the most widely grown variety in the region. It is also known under the names Pansal, Pansalet, Cartoixà, Moll or Pansà blanc although Xarel-lo is by far the most common name. Xarel-lo is a medium sized round grape with a thick amber skin that grows

arellada

Malvasia

to a medium size, slightly lighter bunches and is harvested just after Macabeu. It is grown mostly in central and costal Penedès, but adapts well in most soils at altitudes up to about 300 meters (1000 feet) above sea level, and usually produces an average yield. With its high acidity, aromas and structure, Xarel-lo is considered to be a grape with strong personality that can stand entirely on its own, and give full-bodied wines with great character. Xarel-lo is also one of the grapes that age well in oak, which is used by some producers in their blends—giving toasty, almond and pastry notes to the finish. Quite lovely in my opinion!

Parellada [pəɾəˈʎaðə]

The grapes on the Parellada vine are big and bright green. They have a slightly irregular shape, thick skin and grow in relatively large

bunches. This grape thrives well in most soils, but does best at altitudes between 400-700 meters (1300-2300 feet) above sea level, where the coolness remains later in the day—making the grapes ripen slowly. Parellada normally takes a little longer to mature and is also harvested as the last white variety of the season, with steady and stable returns. The grapes give a fruity and flowery note to the nose, and normally an elegant crisp wine with medium alcohol and high acidity. With its soft floral aromas, the must from Parellada makes a fantastic wine to complement the Cava blends, and also gives some aging potential.

Malvasia / Subirat Parent

Malvasia, called Malmsay in English, is perhaps best known for being the grape usually used to make the famous sweet wine from Ma-

Chardonay

Trepat

deira. It is said to have been cultivated already ancient Greece and is believed to have originated in Asia Minor. The grape grows in large clusters with small yellowish grapes that will blush slightly at full maturity. The grape gives wines with a good flavor composition of sweet and dried fruits and flowers with a moderate acidity and medium alcohol. Malvasia is often called Subirat Parent in the Penedès region, where it is not widely grown at the moment. Though it seems to be acquiring a little more popularity of late.

Chardonnay

This is a grape that has become increasingly popular in Catalonia. The bunches are tight with round small grapes with fine skin. The wines of the Chardonnay grape can vary greatly depending on the growing site, but in Catalo-

nia the Chardonnay usually gives aromatic and full-bodied wines with high acidity and good alcohol. The vine buds very early in the spring and can easily be damaged by frost. Chardonnay is ripe and ready to be harvested in mid-August and is among the first grapes to be picked at harvest.

Trepat

Trepat buds early but takes a long time to mature, and is therefore among the last to be harvested. Trepat grows in relatively large, bright blue or almost purple bunches ,and is strong and durable in nature. The grapes from Trepat may, under current regulations only be used for the production of rosé Cava, and because of this it is the only grape that is subject to restrictions when it comes to use. Trepat is a wonderful grape that offers fruity wines with medium alcohol and balanced acidity. When it comes to sparkling wine this grape is quite unique for the area and gives a very special rosé that I definitely recommend you to try if you ever get the chance.

Monastrell

It is said that Monastrell was the first grape to be used when sparkling wines were first made in Spain, but this has changed and in recent years its use has decreased a lot. The Monastrell vine thrives in most soils and gives moderate yields. The bunches are medium sized and somewhat airy, with small blue round and firm grapes. Monastrell gives full-bodied wines with a relatively high alcohol content and balanced acidity and is often used in blends for rosé Cava as it provides must with intense colour.

Garnacha

Garnacha is one of the most common grape varieties worldwide and is also known as Grenache, Aragonese, Giro, Gironet, Lledoner, Tintilla and Navalcarnero. The grapes are medium sized with a nice skin, and grow in dense, pretty and very classic shaped blue clusters, just as one imagines grapes on a vine. It requires lots of sun, takes a long time to mature, and produces medium-sized yields. The grape is not among the most common in Cava production but provides balanced, fresh and aromatic fruity wines with high alcohol content, ideal for rosé wines.

Monastrell

Pinot noir

Pinot Noir blooms early in the spring and is accordingly, like chardonnay, sensitive to frost. Its bunches are compact with small dark blue grapes. Pinot noir produces the best results in cooler climates where it gives grapes with a nice acidity. For this reason, some producers have started test-plantings of pinot noir at higher altitudes which has partly to do with global warming. Pinot noir is not one of the traditional Cava grapes but was approved for the production of rosé Cava in 1998 and it was only as late as the 2007 harvest that Pinot noir was allowed for production of white Cava. Since then Pinot noir has experienced an increasing popularity and many houses now make both rosé and white Cavas from the grape to the consumers' delight.

Pruning Freixenet

Harvest

Traditional method

There are several methods that can be used for the production of sparkling wine, but the traditional method is indisputably the one that gives wines the most complex character, and in my opinion, the highest quality.

It was in the Champagne region in France that the method was developed. This way of making sparkling wine is very time consuming—requiring both reflection and accuracy. Great care, experience and expertise are of paramount importance for the quality of the final product.

The harvest – La vendimia

Production of quality wines, regardless of variety, always begins in the vineyard. The final product is, as in many other cases, entirely dependent on the raw material. Cava producers

therefore invest a lot of time through the year in tending and taking care of the vineyards and its vines. To prune the vines and remove unwanted shoots and keep the vineyards free from pests and vermin is hard work.

In late March, the first vines begin to bud, and by May they are in full bloom. About 100 days after flowering, you can usually bet that it is time for the harvest, although this varies a little depending on how the summer has been. Each grape variety is harvested at exactly the right time so the producer will be able to get as good a must as possible from the pressing. Sometimes, especially among smaller farmers, harvesting is done by night since the cooler temperatures make it easier to avoid oxidation and retain the aromas of the grape until they reach the pressing.

harvest by hand

BRAUD

Harvest by machine

The grapes can be harvested by hand or by machine. But since many Cava producers are very careful and fussy about their vines and wine, they often use harvest workers to pick the ripe grapes bunch by bunch. Although today's machines are very advanced indeed, they pose a higher risk of damaging the grapes.

When picked, the grapes are always taken as quickly as possible to the press since the goal is to have the grapes as fresh and newly picked as possible. Producers that chose to pick their grapes by hand usually use boxes holding 25 kilograms (55 Ibs) of grapes for the harvest. These boxes are stacked on trailers for transport to the presses at the winery. The reason for using such small boxes is to prevent squashing. If loaded in bigger quantities, the grapes at the bottom of the crate would be crushed and then start to oxidize before the grapes could reach the presses. Again, all is done to get the grapes as fresh as possible to the presses.

The maximum quantity of grapes that a producer is allowed to harvest, from each hectare (2,5 acres) of vineyard is 12 tonnes (1.2 kg per square meter or 2,4 Ibs/1 sq ft) but most producers take far less in order to secure the fine quality of the grapes.

The pressing – Prensado

Each load that enters the press is taken care of promptly in order to have the must as fresh as possible. Each grape variety is, of course, pressed separately from different vineyards' produce to keep certain special flavour. The pressing can be performed in several ways but two methods are most common, one older method and one very modern.

Old press

Seeds and stems

The older presses used are made of wood, where the grapes are emptied into a large round or square crate with a thin wooden frame made of splints and covered with a solid lid. When the crate is full, the lid gently presses the grapes, making the juice flow through the cracks in the wooden crate and down into a tank at a lower level. The more modern presses are so-called pneumatic and consist of a large stainless steel cylindrical tank where a rubber balloon slowly inflates under pressure and, in a very gentle way, pushes the grapes out against the sides of the tank, making them burst and spilling their must.

Whichever method, it is only the first careful pressing that is used for the production of Cava. The current regulations state that only 100 liters (22 gallons) of must is allowed to be pressed from 150 kilograms (330 lbs) of grapes, which is equivalent to 66.6 percent of the total amount that could possibly be pressed from the grapes. In other terms, 100 kilograms (220 lbs) of grapes will give 73 liters (16 gallons) of must, which will end up as 66 liters (14,5 gallons) of base wine for Cava. The musts from later pressings are used or sold to other winemakers for the production of Marc, which is the Catalonian version of the Italian grappa.

Vinification – Vinificación

When the grapes have been pressed the must is usually transferred to stainless steel tanks, where the base wines are to be produced. Creating a base wine is done by adding yeast, after which the first fermentation begins. In the stainless steel tanks, the temperature can

Tanks

The lab

be controlled and is usually kept between 13 to 18 C (55-64 F) depending on the grape and the producer. The use of oak barrels is also possible for the first fermentation but then the nature and style of the final Cava will be quite different since the oak gives aromas and structure to the final product. It is also rather more difficult to control the temperature in oak barrels, although this can be done. The reason why the producers desire to control the temperature during fermentation is mainly because lower temperatures preserve better the fruitiness and freshness in the base wine, which is often desirable. After this first fermentation that takes about 20 days, the grape must have been converted into a base wine that contains from 9.5 to 11.5 volume percent of alcohol.

Blending – Cupada

When the initial fermentation is completed the house normally has several grape specific base wines at disposal. With these, the producer can blend a so-called cuvée, which is a mixture of base wines which together makes up a blend that reflects the style and aging potential sought for the particular individual Cava. A very common and popular cuvee for Cava is made up of one third each of the three traditional grapes Xarel-lo, Parellada and Macabeu, but the different blends made by the houses will, of course, take all kinds of forms.

There is usually a group of persons within the company, all with a long experience in the area of blending that makes the cuvees for the company's portfolio. The blending requires a sound knowledge of the base wines characteristics,

Bottle with ice plug

When the base wines are bottled, a carefully calculated mix of yeast and sugar is added and it is this mixture that makes the second fermentation within the bottle possible. The amount of yeast and sugar that is added to each bottle is carefully calculated, and the amount of carbon dioxide that develops will give a total pressure in the bottle of about 6 bars (which is the same pressure as in a truck tyre). The amount of yeast cells added to the base wine is about 1 200 000 cells/ml or 30 million cells in 1 fl oz. (1 ml=0,04 fl oz), this equals 900 million cells per standard bottle. It is incredible, I know!

After the mixture has been added, the bottle is sealed with a crown cap. Also cork with a staple can be used, but the use of a cork is most common for bottles that are to be stored for a long time, such as Gran Reservas, or for various kinds of prestige cuvées.

Stacking – Rima

When the bottles have been filled with their content of base wine, yeast and sugar, all the bottles are moved down into the cellars to rest. In order to utilize the space as effectively as possible the bottles are often stacked wrap-around, and this way they come to make up large walls in the cellars. Here in the dark, they are then left to undergo the second fermentation, and to ripen and age.

It is during this second fermentation that the bubbles are created. The yeast will consume the sugar and the waste products, so to speak, are alcohol and carbonic acid. When the yeast has

their aging ability and, of course, a good familiarity with the particular house style and the types of Cavas that are supposed to make up the portfolio. It is not an easy task to predict how the wines will taste after aging and many consider it a form of art to be able to blend a fine quality Cava.

Bottling – Tiraje

When the blending team has agreed on a desired cuvée, the bottling begins. From this moment on the wine is to stay in the very same bottle until the moment comes when the Cava is to be enjoyed. However, before it's time for the bottle to be shipped off to the store where we can buy it, it first has to go through many time-consuming steps that will finally transform the still wine in the bottle to Cava.

Pupitres

Bottles in rima

consumed all the available sugar, it will naturally die and sink to the bottom of the bottle. When the second fermentation has reached its end, the alcohol percentage has increased somewhat and is usually between 11 and 12 volume percent.

The traditional underground cellars are perfect places for storage since they hold a steady temperature between 15-17 C (59-63 F). Whatever the weather or season may be above ground, the temperature in the cellars is not affected. This makes it possible for the Cava to mature slowly in perfect conditions. The time the Cava is left to mature in the cellars depends on the type that is desired. The most common Cavas sold are among those which have been on the lees the shortest time, where the minimum is nine months. Many producers choose to store

their bottles longer though, to get the slightly more complex flavours to come forward. After 15 months of storage the Cava is allowed to be called Reserva and after 30 months it can be given the title Gran Reserva. Later in this book, we will go more into the details and regulations regarding different styles and shapes of Cava.

Riddling – Removido

When the base wine has undergone the second fermentation and the aging in the cellars is complete, the only thing left is to get the yeast out of the bottle. This can be done either manually or mechanically. In traditional manual *removido*, as it is called in Spanish, the bottles are fixed horizontally into wooden or concrete stands called *a*. These pupitres hold a total of 60 bottles, 6 in width and 10 in

Manual riddling

Semi manual riddling

height. From their horizontal starting position the bottles are rotated with a flick one eighth of a turn, one or two days apart every time, while the bottle is also pushed inwards into the cone-shaped hole in the wooden stands. This allows the bottle by the end of the procedure, to stand almost vertically on the cork. With these shaky rotations of the bottle, the dead yeast cells slide down the side and neck of the bottle and collect at the bottom on the inside of the crown cap or cork. All in all, this process usually takes around two weeks but that obviously depends on how many days apart you choose to shake the bottles. This hand-shaking of the bottles is a very time consuming and costly process, so that the method is currently used very sparingly by most producers, although a few still do this through their whole range of cuvées.

Nowadays, the process has been automated through the use of so-called gyropalates. The producers, who have always been innovative, invented the gyropalates in the early nineteen-seventies, and have since been using them with very good results. The bottles are packed in large metal crates, or packed with special separators and bands, approximately five hundred bottles in each unit, which are then attached to a hydraulic arm. The machine then shakes and turns the bottles according a programmed schedule which completes the bottles in all from forty-eight hours up to a week. The gyropalates make the process easier and more efficient for the medium-sized producers and have been a precondition for some of the larger houses to reach the enormous quantities of bottles they currently produce.

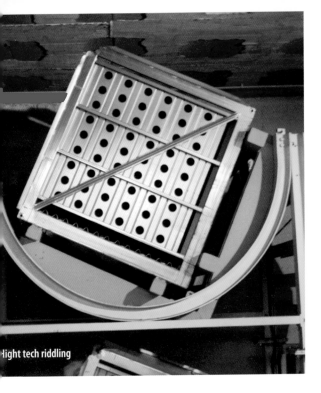
High tech riddling

Manual degorgement

By far the biggest producer, Freixenet, has also developed their own gyropallets which, in combination with a special yeast, has reduced the time further with regard to the riddling. One hour is all it takes with their specialized equipment. This is possible because the special yeast they produced is crystal-shaped and does not stick to the inside of the glass bottle, as regular yeasts tend to do. These gyropalettes do not shake the bottles but just straighten them up from a horizontal position to a position where they stand on the head. It is all incredibly simple but extremely fast and effective. Consider that they also produce about 130 million bottles of Cava annually.

Degorgement – Degüelle

When the bottles have been turned on their heads and the yeast has been accumulated in the bottom of the bottleneck, it is time to remove the lees. Although this can be done by hand it is nowadays more common to do it mechanically. However, there are obstacles to making the degorgement by machine and that is if a cork with a staple has been used instead of a crown cap. In these cases, the removal of the lees must be done by hand. Then one holds the bottle, still upside down, and in one steady movement turns the bottle so the neck points upward while loosening the Staple, making the cork pop out and with it the lees are ejected by the pressure inside. This is all very labour intensive indeed but still the traditional way of doing it.

When the bottles are sealed with crown caps there is a much easier way. The bottles, which rest with the cap down are moved in the same

43

Adding dosage

increase the alcohol content by more than 0.5 volume percent.

Making Cava by the steps that have just been de-scribed is only allowed in four bottle sizes; the half bottle, the standard bottle, magnums (double bottles) and Jeroboams (double magnum). That is to say that the Cava in these bottles has gone through all the aforementioned steps. However, after addition of the dosage, it is permitted to transfer the Cava to bottles of other sizes. The types that are then allowed are the smaller Piccolo, as well as the larger models over three litres, Rehoboam, Methuselem, Salamanzar, Balthazar, Nebuchadnezzar and Solomon. Permission to carry out these transfers is of course regulated and controlled by the Consejo Regulador.

position to a bath of refrigerant that freezes the neck of the bottle only, making an ice plug that encapsulates the lees that collected there. The bottles are then transported into a machine that turns the bottles one by one and snaps the cap so that the ice plugs fly out. A simple procedure if you have the right equipment and this has made it possible to increase the productivity also in this part of the process.

Dosage – licor de expediciónn

After the bottles have been degorged, it's time to add the dosage, to fill up the bottle to the original volume and in doing so, determine the style of Cava to be made: *brut nature, brut, extra seco, seco, semi-seco* or *dulce*. The dosage is a mixture of base wine and sugar, or grape juice or another cuvee. Even the use of grape distillate is allowed, as long as the addition does not

> **The traditional bottle sizes**
> As a curiosity may it be mentioned that many of the names are taken from biblical kings, although the reason for this remains unknown.[1]
>
> Picolo or quarter bottle – 20 cl
> Half Bottle – 375 cl
> Bottle – 750 cl
> Magnum – 1.5 litres (2 bottles)
> Jeroboam – 3 litres (four bottles)
> Rehoboam – 4.5 litres (6 bottles)
> Methuselah – 6 litres (8 bottles)
> Salamanzar – 9 litres (12 bottles)
> Balthazar – 12 litres (16 bottles)
> Nebuchadnezzar – 15 litres (20 bottles)
> Solomon – 18 litres (24 bottles)

Corking and labeling

After the dosage has been added, the next step is to re-seal the bottle which is done with a cork. Always using high quality corks with the associated seal plaque and steel halter. The seal that is placed between the cork and the steel halter, that is the small metal cap that you see at the top of the cork when you remove the foil from around the neck of the bottle, has become another focus area for many producers. Some houses nowadays often design small works of art for certain Cavas and sometimes even use different caps for each and every type of Cava within the house portfolio. Others houses are not so ambitious and are more than happy to put the house logo on all their products. It is wonderful to see how much work and heart is put in to making each product a special one, right up to such small details. Many Cava lovers have started to collect these seals and store them in specialized frames made just for this purpose. [2]

Looking at the cork you will notice that many of them are made up by two parts. The section at the bottom, that will stay in contact with the Cava is the part with the highest quality. This of course due to the fact that the producers are extremely careful not to use corks that might damage the wine after such a long process. And in my experience, you very seldom come across a cork-damaged Cava or Champagne.

Corking by hand

When the bottle is sealed, the cork is usually put into the neck mechanically and receives at the same moment the small metal seal and its steel halter which ensures that the cork stays securely in place. At the bottom of the cork, you can see the black four-pointed star which is always printed on the bottom of the corks used for Cava.

The neck foil and the front and back labels affixed on the bottle are the last details to be put in place before everything is ready and here there is much information for us consumers to find.

---

[1] If you know the story behind this, please send me an e-mail. I am dying to know.

[2] Personally I make magnets of the ones I like and put them on my fridge

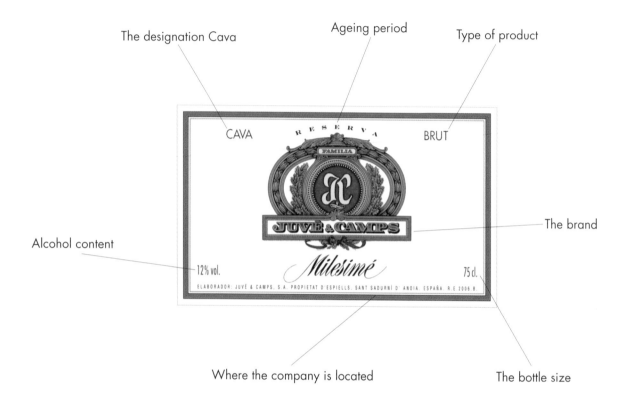

The designation Cava

Ageing period

Type of product

CAVA

RESERVA

BRUT

Alcohol content

12% vol.

The brand

Milésimé

75 cl.

ELABORADOR: JUVÉ & CAMPS, S.A. PROPIETAT D'ESPIELLS, SANT SADURNÍ D' ANOIA, ESPAÑA, R.E.2006.B.

Where the company is located

The bottle size

First and foremost, it should state that it is Cava, clearly marked on the bottle. Also it must name the producer, type of product, strength, volume and what aging class the Cava belongs to, i.e. Cava, Reserva or Gran Reserva should be apparent. The back label can include information on what grapes are included in the cuvée and perhaps some tasting notes so we know what to expect. However, the information on the back label depends on just what the producer wants to highlight about his or her product. In accordance with the Consejo Reguladors regulations, there should always be information about the date of disgorgement on the back label so that we as consumers can decide when we choose to drink the Cava, and also to assure us that the bottle in question has not been standing on some dusty shelf in a shop or warehouse for 10 years before someone sold it to us. This number can be hard to read though since it is sometimes also used as an internal code at the winery and may not always be marked as a clear date although one can always find out by asking the producer.

Can cava age?

For a long time, I wondered why so many people persisted in saying that Cava, as opposed to Champagne, is a perishable wine.

Maybe the reason for this opinion is mainly that the majority of bottles produced, about 90 percent in fact, are young Cavas that are meant to be enjoyed right away, or at least within the year. These young wines are not for saving, so it is easy to think that this is the only truth.

The reality though is that a Cava producer can produce fantastic Gran Reservas if he or she so chooses and most also have the material for doing so. But it is true that all base wines are not suitable for creating sparkling wines that are to age tens of years. There are things to take into careful consideration when aging sparkling wine, like acidity, balance, fruitiness etc. and since Cava can be made from nine different grape varieties, and can be grown in many terroirs over Spain there is the knowledge and experience of the winemaker that

producers have followed in their footsteps. What these long aged Cavas usually have in common is that they are, if not to a hundred percent, at least based on the grape Xarel-lo. The reason for this is not just the fact that it does well as a single grape wine, but studies has also shown that Xarel-lo is the grape to contain the highest level of antioxidants so far measured. These high levels of antioxidants makes the Xarel-lo optimal for ageing. Some people would even argue that it is the best grape to use if you want to age sparkling wine.

I have personally experienced the effect of these antioxidants when comparing, side by side, Cavas and Champagnes from the same vintages. The difference was striking. How these Cavas can stay so young really puzzles me, and for anyone who doubts the potential that lies within Cava, go ahead and do the same comparison.

makes the difference. Producers like Gramona and Recaredo have already proven for many years that Cava can be aged for periods over ten years with fantastic results and more

Did you know that …

The production of Gran Reserva is usually around 2 percent of the total production, while Reserva makes up around 8 percent, annually? This means that no more than one out of ten bottles have over 9 months of ageing.

So even though the predominant tradition or the predominant trend at the moment, at least, is to drink styles that are quite young, there are also wonderful mature Cavas to be had. Luckily the trend to age Cava longer is growing and it is easier today to find Gran Reservas than it was earlier, and with the new category of Cava Paraje Calificado we will most likely see this segment growing in the future.

Cava de Paraje Calificado – the new elite

Cava as mentioned earlier is to the largest extent young, looked at the number of bottles produced. Young does in most cases mean inexpensive and hence Cava has received the reputation of being just that... inexpensive fizz. Although we are many trying to show that Cava is diverse, both when it comes to grapes, styles, ageing and price, it is hard to fight against the perception that the millions of bottles of cheap Cava creates. This has been a headache for the producers and the Consejo Regulador del Cava for a very long time. There has been a will to show that there is also another side to this coin, although less known. The conclusion was that a new classification should be created with strict rules on yields, quality of the vines, ageing, production and more.

In July 2017, the new classification of Cava was official, Cava de Paraje Calificado (CPC), and the first 12 vineyards that passed the requirements presented. This new category will show consumers a new top range of Cavas that represents the land and embodies the soul of the earth where

the vines grow. The standards are set very high and the production will be very limited indeed.

The rules and regulations

The vineyards used must be a small area with vines that are at least ten years old and naturally inspected and approved by the consejo regulador del Cava.

Grapes: All the nine varieties are allowed: *Xarel-lo, Macabeu, Parellada, Malvasia/Subirat Parent, Chardonnay, Garnacha, Monastrell, Trepat* and *Pinot noir.*

Yields: Maximum yield of 8,000 kg/ha (7050 Ibs / acre) and 48 hl/ha (422 imp gal/acre)

Ageing: Minimum 36 months

Style: *Brut, Extra Brut* or *Brut Nature*

Apart from this there are only vintage wines allowed and the wine cannot be acidified, but must have a natural acidity level of 5.5 g/l (1 ounce/1 imp gal) (measured in tartaric).

An extra rule set on the producer is that all CPC-vineyards must be owned by the producer or contracted on long-term lease. The reason for this is that the CPC-Cavas must be one hundred percent traceable.

When the hard facts have been settled and the vineyard and the Cava fills all the criteria, the final Cava is set blind in front of a jury of outside wine judges. Here the Cava is tasted and the winemaker gets the chance to explain why this Cava is a clear expression of the terroir and why this vineyard is unique. Some Cavas tried and failed but here below are the first 12 that made it.

Cava de Paraje Calificado: the pioneers

Producer	Vineyard	Cava
Torelló	Vinyes de Can Martí	Gran Torelló, 225
Recaredo	Turó d'en Mota	Turó d'en Mota
Recaredo	Serral del Vell	Serral del Vell
Alta Alella	Vallcirera	Mirgin
Juvé y Camps	La Capella	La Capella
Freixenet (Can Sala)	Can Sala	Casa Sala
Codorníu	La Pleta	Finca La Pleta
Codorníu	El Tros Nou	Finca El Tros Nou
Codorníu	La Fideuera	Finca La Fideuera
Vins el Cep	Can Prats	Claror
Gramona	Font de Jui	Enoteca, Cellar Batlle, III Lustros
Castellroig	Terroja	Sabaté i Coca

SWEET OR DRY, YOUNG OR OLD?

Perhaps you think that the title above should be reversed, because taste-wise it feels more natural to go from dry to sweet. But if you look at the development historically our preferences as consumers have gone from sweet to drier styles.

Historically, sugar was a luxury commodity for a long time and which may, perhaps, be one of the reasons why we preferred sweeter drinks up to the beginning of the 1900's. Some say that it was the English who started the trend of demanding drier sparkling wines and that this spread throughout Europe and beyond. Today the trend seems to have spread to all corners of the world, only leaving Russia and the eastern European neighbours as its last outpost. Another aspect of this trend with increasingly drier sparkling wines is that it puts a higher pressure on the producer when it comes to quality and skill. This is due to the fact that sugar, that acts as a flavour enhancer, is added much more restrictively. The grapes that make up the base wine then need to be able to stand on their own and the cuvees need to be blended to perfection, since the sugar that may mask minor flaws in some cases is taken out of the equation.

Even though the trend in sparkling wines, made by traditional method is now dry or even super dry, there are still sweeter styles to be found and they all have a place to fill when it comes to combinations with food and personal tastes.

The driest style we can find according to the regulatory framework is *brut nature*. Cavas made in this style may contain up to three grams of sugar per liter but no sugar may be added in the dosage. How does it work, you might wonder? Well during the second fermentation when sugar and yeast have been added, there is some sugar left after the fermentation has come to an end. The yeast simply cannot consume every little sugar molecule which means that you can still find residual sugar in the finished product.

Extra brut is second in line and slightly sweeter, even if sweet is not the right word to describe this style. These are very dry indeed and contain a maximum of six grams of sugar per litre and here it is allowed to add sugar in the dosage. Both the *brut nature* and *extra brut* are styles that with their super-crisp character are excellent as an aperitif, just as they are or served together with lightly salted chips. If you want to eat anything with these two styles, gently spiced seafood is a classic match or, if you want to give yourself a treat, oysters.

The most common style we find in our shops, and certainly the best-seller at present is the *brut*. Here you can find up to 12 grams of sugar per

litre, but these are still perceived as dry on the tongue. Among this style it is much easier to find good "food-Cavas" in my opinion. This is due to the fact that we often have some sweetness in our food, even if we are talking about main courses, and a well-balanced *brut* goes very well with many types of food and also meat dishes. Of course it will not match all dishes but, on the other hand, no wine will.

If you go further along the sweetness scale you will find *extra seco* next in line and here it is easy to get a bit confused. This because Seco means "dry", so extra seco actually means "extra dry" but it is just here that we are starting to touch on the sweeter styles. To understand this, one can divide the scale in two parts. Firstly one older original part that reflects the styles the first Cavas were made, consisting of *extra seco, seco,*

semi-seco and *dulce*. Among these *extra seco* was certainly a very dry Cava indeed, while *seco* was dry, *semi-seco* was half dry and *dulce* was the sweet one. So far, everything is pretty clear. The second part consists of the styles that were born when the demand grew for dry sparkling wines. *Extra seco* was no longer dry enough, so the sugar levels in the dosage were reduced and the drier brut came into the picture, followed by extra brut and finally so dry it will ever get, with brut nature. What historically seems quite obvious is now at first glance a bit confusing.

The slightly sweeter Cavas, like *seco* and *semi-seco*, are perceived today as being quite sweet. *Seco*, which we would classify as half dry, works superbly as an appetizer, while the sweeter *semi-seco* can be a very nice companion to desserts. *Semi Seco* contains between 33 to 50 grams of

sugar per litre, which is quite sweet. Consumers in large do not request Cava sweeter than semi seco but there is still some made under the style called *Dulce*, which also means sweet. *Dulce* has only a minimum amount in terms of sugar, 50 grams per litre and is definitely a wine that should be served with sweet desserts. It can be very difficult to find these sweet Cavas on the market since not many producers have a *dulce* in their standard portfolio. The house of Gramona is one of the few that make a high quality, well-aged *dulce* that you may be lucky enough to get your hands on without travelling to Spain. Jaume Gramona also told me a story behind the company's sweet Cava and why it is a classic that will probably stay on forever in the standard portfolio of the house. It is a very good story indeed and if you have the luck to meet him, perhaps he will tell you the story too.

Cava doesn't only get its character from the base wine and the amount of sugar that is added in the dosage, but also from the time it has been aged in the cold cellars. That is to say, how long it has been left to lie on its side, still in contact with the yeast that has done its work during the second fermentation, creating the bubbles and then dying. However, after falling

Brut Nature: maximum 3 g sugar / l and no added sugar.
Extra brut: maximum 6 g sugar / l
Brut: maximum 12 g sugar / l
Extra seco: 12-17 g sugar / l
Seco: 17-32 g sugar / l
Semi-seco: 32-50 g sugar / l
Dulce: more than 50 g / l

to the bottom of the bottle, the yeast will still be contributing to the development of aromas in the wine.

Cava has three age classes if you like, as we mentioned above. The most common is just called *Cava*, the slightly older is called *Reserva* and the oldest *Gran Reserva*, which are left 9, 15 and 30 months with the yeast still in the bottle to age. There is of course also Cava Paraje Calificado that has to age more than 36 months, but it is so much more than about ageing. *(See earlier chapter)*.

The most common Cava that is aged at least nine months is the type that we most often come across in the shop. These young Cavas are light and fresh in style and are not supposed to be stored at home with us consumers

for any longer period of time. Although the producers claim that these Cavas are more or less perishable and should be enjoyed as soon as possible, I have had several bottles of this type that have survived well in my small cellar for at least two years. The common Cavas aged for at least nine months are found in all types of styles when it comes to sweetness, from brut nature to dulce and stand for 90 percent of all Cava production.

The *Reserva* is aged for at least 15 months, becoming more golden yellowish in colour and also more complex in its taste. There are usually clearer notes of bread in the aroma and flavour and usually some ripe fruit in the *Reservas*, unlike the younger Cavas that have more of the fresh, acidic fruit to the nose and on the tongue. The after-taste in these slightly older Cavas is longer and rounded in nature and they are produced in all styles of sweetness from the brut nature to dulce, although most commonly in the drier styles. These *Reservas* can usually be stored in your basement or cellar for a while and are not as sensitive as the younger Cavas in this regard.

The *Gran Reserva* is the Cava that has been stored the longest of all and can be described as the "queen of Cava". During its time in the cellars it often grows a great darker golden colour and develops soft notes of toasted bread, honey, almonds and ripe fruit. Although this type must be stored at least 30 months in accordance to the regulations, there are many producers who age their *Gran Reserva* much much longer. Due to the composition and long slow ageing of these wines at the producer, it is usually said that they can also be kept and aged by us consumers to a greater extent then the other styles. Although you could certainly keep the *Gran Reserva* in storage in your own cellar, basement or cupboard, it may be quite difficult to let something so good go untouched for a long time.

The production of *Gran Reserva* is allowed only for the styles brut nature, extra brut and brut according to Consejo Regulador's regulations. So, even if a producer would age there *seco* or *dulce* for more then 30 months, they still could not call it Gran Reserva.

Rosé Cava, or *rosado* as it is called in Spain in general, is also counted as one of the four

typical styles and has become increasingly popular over the years. Commonly used grapes are Monastrell, red Garnacha, Pinot noir and Trepat, where Trepat is allowed to be used only for this purpose. These grapes typically provide a fantastic fresh fruitiness of red berries, which is also common in other wines of rosé type but, again, the types of grapes used and styles on the Cava vary from producer to producer. When it comes to aging potential at your home, most would say that this is a type that is at its best when enjoyed quite young and is nothing that you should save for a long time in the racks. This is because rosado has a tendency to lose its fruitiness during longer storage and also its beautiful colour that turns more orange with time. But there are of course beautiful Gran Reservas also in this category, but not very common.

THE WORLD'S GREATEST BUBBLES

Even though Cava has a long history, it was only in the late 1900's and now after the start of the new millennia that it has grown so radically in the international market. The expanding Cava trend is becoming evident in very many countries and you meet more people every day who have started to grow an interest for these Spanish bubbles. Furthermore, it is not only during a vacation or weekend in the Barcelona area that people have learned about Cava, because now, the trend is spreading by itself out in the world market. Cava bars are no longer to be found only in Barcelona.

We have like with so many other wines realised that Cava has a unique taste and character that is good in so many ways. The wine is diverse and can be served with all kinds of food and even here in our small country of Sweden, any restaurant with some self-respect has at least one Cava on the wine list. This is also made a lot easier since really good Cava is so much more accessible now than it was 30 years ago. The number of producers has increased from 82 in 1980 to 235 in 2016, which is an increase of almost 300 percent in 35 years. Naturally, all these producers have pushed up the total

production and also increased the range available in the market. As mentioned earlier, the all-time high record of Cava bottles sold across the world was reached with 245 million bottles in 2016. [3]

The statistics tell of a success story with over 120 countries importing Cava; from Guadalupe to China everyone wants to taste the Spanish gold. However, it is Germany, the United Kingdom, Belgium and the United States that are by far the largest fans around and have been so for some years. Together they bought two thirds of the entire international sales in 2016, almost half of the total sales. But all together, we who live outside Spain in their export market, drink a bit more than 60 percent of all Cava sold, while nearly 40 percent stays in Spain. Curiously, almost the reverse numbers apply to the French and their Champagne, since over 50 percent of this is drunk within France.

Looking at the English-speaking countries, the US seems to experiencing a rising Cava trend the last years. Since 2011 the import of Cava has grown by 23 percent in the country. The sales in Canada and Australia are also pointing

---

[3] And hopefully the sales will be even higher in years to come

up, while the UK seems to have fallen in love with Prosecco, leaving the Cava imports to fall.

What is interesting and very good news is that the export of quality Cava, Reserva and Gran Reserva, is growing steadily. This will hopefully help with changing the look on Cava as cheap bubbles in the long run. As will the growing production of organic and biodynamic Cava, that seems to increase rapidly.

Cava is spreading and more people are getting interested in these fantastic bubbles every day. The fact that these Spanish bubbles are a bit less pricy than Champagne and still just as interesting is, of course, a great advantage when conquering the world although now we are also learning not to compare the two, which is great since Cava wants to be appreciated for its own qualities.

Did you know that ...

In Spain, the people prefer their Cava drier than other countries and drink almost 80 percent of all the Cava brut or brut nature that is produced. While the rest of us stand for the consumption of the semi-sweet. More than 50 percent of all Cava consumed outside Spain is semi-seco or seco.

CAVA AND FOOD, A LOVE STORY

If you ask anyone living in Catalonia, they will tell you that Cava goes with all types of food. That may be as it may since I have not tried everything so I can't be sure, but I do agree that Cava goes with most kinds of food.

I have so many memories that involve food and Cava and one of the real highlights was actually the summer I was writing the first edition of this book. My husband and I were invited to our fantastic neighbours for some moules marinères, mussels cooked in white wine one of our favourite dishes in fact, so we accepted with delight. We happily brought a Cava brut nature that we had lying in the fridge and sat down on the neighbours' little veranda. Oh Gosh! what a sensation! We ate mussels and garlic bread and drank Cava like there was no tomorrow. And when we were done, there was neither a single clam in the pan nor a drop of Cava left in the bottle! We all agreed that we had to do it all again soon.

Another memory is from one of our friends wedding reception where a Cava Gran Reserva was served with the main course which consisted of fried perch-pike, roasted root vegetables, lemon hollandaise and bacon-wrapped green asparagus. This was also a fantastic match and the Cava's powerful character took on the role as main course wine perfectly. It complemented the salty bacon and soft solid perch-pike and, at the same time, it broke through and balanced up the lemon hollandaise. The bride and groom were happy, and I was more than satisfied, since the Cava in question was one of my personal favourites and it was I who had suggested that they should try it.

When you look at old traditions, you often get the feeling that sparkling wines generally should be drunk as an aperitif or, at most, enjoyed together with seafood. I find that to be a bit boring and playing it a bit too safe. Of course, many sparkling wines make a splendid aperitif, Cava included, because sparkling wine has an amazing ability to get people into that great party mood. It also tickles your taste buds and makes you a bit hungry, but with a little food to go with the Cava it can grow to another dimension.

Looking at the Catalan cuisine you find fantastic seafood, of course, but there is so much more variety to be had. Here you have a cuisine with very strong flavours together with botifarra, olives, Jamón, or other cured hams and also much richer food. The Catalans are not afraid to combine these powerful tastes with their favourite bubbles, which are usually the very dry styles like extra brut and brut nature. This same habit is catching on with the consumers in Europe and the rest of the world who are now growing fonder of drier fizz.

Cava and the four flavours

So why is it that Cava goes well with so many types of food? To answer this question, we have to look at the flavour components in Cava and how these react with the basic flavours of food; salty, sour, bitter and sweet, because it has very much to do with the chemistry.

Cava as a wine, has a very high acidity, sweetness depending on style, sometimes a hint of bitterness and very importantly it has carbon dioxide that helps to clean and refresh the palate after every bite of food. This is more important than one would think when it comes to the combination of wine and food, especially together with fat and sweet foodstuffs, where a fresh finish helps to lighten the perception of the dish.

Cava is also full of aromas like, apple, pear, bread, honey, almonds and so on, but taking these into account is not the hardest issue when matching food and wine. The one main thing we do need to think about when it comes to aromas is that the complexity and fullness of the Cava must match the complexity of the dish. For example, light uncomplicated seafood likes the company of a light uncomplicated Cava while a heavy meat dish with many flavours in both meat, sauce, vegetables and garnish, needs a complex full-bodied Cava to match the versatility. However, apart from the fact that the food and the Cava need to balance when it comes to aromas, we need to focus on the four basic flavours because it is here that things can get tricky.

Salty

Wines are normally never salty but are often matched with salty foodstuffs like anchovy, sauces, cured meats, chips, crisps and so on. Salt has a remarkable effect to cushion the other flavours and to bring out the aromas in both food and wine.

Salt will lessen the effect of the acidity in the wine and bring out the aromas. Try a nice Cava with lightly salted potato crisps; it is truly a fantastic match. Salty food will also lessen the sensation of bitterness in the wine, if there is any, just as sweetness in wine will also lessen the saltiness of the food.

Sour

Cava is by style a very acidic wine indeed which gives us an impression of freshness. Also, many things we eat have a high concentration of acidity like, lemon, vinegar, many types of cheese and crème fraîche. When acidity in wine meets acidity in food, a chemical phenomenon occurs called adaptation. When these two meet, we perceive the taste as less acid. You can easily try this adaptation effect by doing an experiment. Take a sip of your Cava feeling the acidity on the side of your tongue, then bite in a lemon and taste the Cava again. It's a fun experiment to be sure.

Acidity also has a calming effect on bitterness, while it accentuates sweetness. So, if you have heavily grilled food or salads where you sense bitterness, the acidity of the Cava will smoothen it. Equally, if you have a sweet desert, you will most probably find that the Cava makes the dessert seem even sweeter, while you will find

the acidity of the wine more vivid. This may result in you finding the combination extra fresh especially since you have the carbon dioxide to refresh your palate.

Bitter

The taste of bitter is not one always to be appreciated when found in the wrong places. You find it naturally in many types of salads, over-grilled meats, citrus peels and herbs. When bitter tastes in food and wine (or other drinks such as beer) are combined, the sensation of the bitterness is enhanced, which is often not pleasant. However, since Cava is very seldom very bitter, there is nothing to provoke the bitterness in the food it meets, and since we have the acidity in the Cava to calm the bitterness, as you will remember from the previous section, our Cava is usually a good friend to the bitterness in your food.

Sweet

Sweetness is something we normally like since it sends a signal to the brain that this foodstuff is likely to contain lots of energy, which the body needs, although we sometimes give our bodies too much of the good sweet stuff.

Sweetness is of course most obvious in desserts even though you will find it in many other foods as well, for example foie gras, fried onions and baked tomatoes to mention a few. As mentioned before, you can find Cava with all types of sweetness from extra seco, where it starts to get noticeably sweet to the really sweet dulce.

When it comes to sweet food meeting sweet wine we have the adaptation phenomenon once again. So if you eat a sweet cake with a sweet wine you will find the combination less sweet. It sounds strange I know but it's true, they balance out somehow. So if you choose a slightly sweet Cava to your dessert you will not only find that the combination balances, but you will also have a refreshing sensation thanks to the carbon dioxide - a wonderful win-win situation! The Cava that is also very high in acidity, no matter whether it is dry or sweet, will also push its freshness a little further in this situation, so you will get that extra twist.

So you see, no matter what you eat, there is most likely a Cava that would make a perfect match. You just need to think about balancing the aromas, light Cava with light food, and then the sweetness of your food, if you want that to balance too. All the other things, the Cava's natural characteristics will smoothen out for you.

I have been experimenting with Cava and food pairings for some years now and found some absolute hits like the ones I mentioned in the beginning of this chapter. Apart from the mussels and brut nature, I think you should try a little more matured Cava, perhaps a Gran Reserva, with a little lighter meat, some roasted potatoes and a creamy mushroom sauce, rich enough I know but it is lovely. I also think that you should try a little sweeter Cava together with some fresh fruits like melon or strawberries with a little vanilla cream, for example. And one of my absolute favourites is actually a dessert Cava made from one 100 percent malvasia grapes, and with a dosage of a sweet sherry-like

wine, which gives the Cava an amazing depth and a very special character that pairs wonderfully with crema catalana and crispy toffee biscuits.

The list of good combinations is long but the fact remains that I have been pairing Cava with almost everything at home because I like to see what happens. My advice to you is to do the same and explore on your own, for it is ever so much fun. Furthermore, the knowledge of others and good advice are always helpful, but they may also have missed something or maybe you are of a complete different opinion. And if you go experimenting on your own, perhaps you'll find that fantastic combination that you can treat your friends to next time you have them over. Try it! What have you got to lose?

RECIPES

Here are some of my favourite recipes that I think are a good match for Cava. Of course, you do not have to follow them slavishly because all food is better if you put your own touch to it.

MOULES MARINIÈRES

This is one of my husband's many parade recipes and can be served both as a starter or main course. This particular recipe is calculated as a starter for four people but if you would rather serve it as a main course for the same number of people you just have to double everything and accompany it with plenty of fresh good garlic bread. This is how we tend to eat it.

INGREDIENTS

1 net of mussels (½ kilo)

3 large shallots

30 cl white wine

three cloves of garlic

Parsley, to your liking

1 tablespoon of lobster stock

DO LIKE THIS

1. Wash the mussels in cold water and take out the ones that do not close.

2. Chop the shallots and garlic into small pieces.

3. Heat a few tablespoons of oil and a knob of butter in a large saucepan and fry the onion and garlic until golden.

4. Pour in the wine and the stock and boil up, add the mussels and cook until they have opened up.

5. Sprinkle the parsley over the mussels and serve immediately! This recipe is a piece of cake and still so fantastically good.

To drink? A well-chilled Cava brut nature, preferably a classical one made from Xarel-lo, Parellada and Macabeu. I do have a soft spot for the classic grapes I must admit.

MOULES CATALANES

These mussels we actually tried the first time in the big restaurant street of Reims in the Champagne district. After returning home, we made our own version which has become one of our favourites. This dish is a bit more filling, and perhaps best suited as a main course. With mussels and some good bread to soak up the sauce, you can feed four hungry friends with this without any problems.

INGREDIENTS

2 nets of mussels (1 kilo)

3 shallots

4 tomatoes

2 spicy sausages, like chorizo

3 tablespoons of crème fraîche

30 cl of cream

Parsley, according to your liking

½ a fresh chili

DO LIKE THIS

1. Chop the shallots and chili finely and cut the tomatoes in half wedges.

2. Heat a little oil and butter in a large saucepan and fry the onions soft together with the chili. Add the chopped tomatoes, cream and crème fraîche and let it all simmer for a few minutes.

3. Slice the sausages into half centimeter-thick slices and fry them in a pan while the tomato and cream mixture is simmering in the pot.

4. Add the mussels to the tomato and crème sauce and boil under a lid until the mussels have opened up.

5. Add the sausage and the chopped parsley to the mussels, stir gently and serve right away with fresh bread.

To drink? A well-aged Cava Gran Reserva, since the body of the Cava and the larger spectra of aromas will match the slightly complex mussel dish and make a great match. And don't forget to choose your favourite grape composition.

TORTILLA DE PATATAS

This dish, I encountered the first time when I was studying in England and had two girls from San Sebastian (Basque Country) in the same dorm. They basically lived on Tortilla de Patatas and carried home copious amounts of eggs and potatoes. This is a great dish that can serve as a snack for many, as in the student corridor in England, or as lunch for four people with a little salad to go along with it. This is a basic recipe but you can certainly spice it up with any seasoning. Garlic or chilli work well and also a little onion chopped up with the potato when it is almost cooked gives a richer tortilla.

INGREDIENTS

4 eggs.

½ kg potatoes

Olive oil

Salt

DO LIKE THIS

1. Peel the potatoes and cut them into small cubes and dry them with paper. Pour plenty of oil into a frying pan so it covers the bottom and goes up the edge about one-half to one centimeter. Add the potatoes when the oil is warm but be careful so that the oil does not get too warm, it should never smoke.

2. When the potatoes have a golden colour, you just lift out them out with a slotted spoon. Save the oil, because you can use it again next time you make tortilla de patatas.

3. Whisk the eggs and add some salt. Add the fried potatoes and stir. Here you can choose if you want the potatoes in whole pieces or if you want to mash them a little and get a more mixed tortilla.

4. Heat the pan again and add a little more oil if the pan seems dry. Add the potato mixture and cook on low heat until the bottom of the cake seems to have settled. You can lift a little of the edge and see if the bottom has become golden brown. The top of the tortilla will still not have solidified entirely but that is how it should be. Bring a plate that is large enough to cover the entire pan and goes a little out over the pan's edges. Place the plate as a lid over the pan and, taking a firm grip around the edges with two pot holders, hold your breath, brace yourself, and turn the whole thing upside-down, so you flip the tortilla on to the plate instead. Now, slide the tortilla back down into the pan again. Fry it on this other side a little while, but not for long, because you don't want to get it all dry. Put the finished tortilla on a plate and eat it warm, lukewarm or cold.

To drink? On its own the tortilla de patatas goes well with the brut nature or brut, since the tortilla is quite mild in its complexion. If you spice it up with onions, garlic and other spices or have it together with meats and sauces, you need to think about the balance of the drink and food together.

CREMA CATALANA WITH CRISPY TOFFEE BISCUITS

This is a wonderful dessert that most people like. My experience is that kids also appreciate this dessert. Perhaps it's because of the easy vanilla and crème taste.

This is calculated for four people, even though the biscuits are often enough for more - or you may just have some left over for later.

INGREDIENTS

Crema Catalana

1 vanilla pod

6 egg yolks

170 grams of granulated sugar

10 cl milk

40 cl whipping cream

white table sugar

DO LIKE THIS

1. Start by setting the oven at 150 degrees Celsius.

2. Cut the vanilla pod lengthwise and scrape out the seeds. Put seeds and the whole pod in a saucepan with the milk, cream and the granulated sugar.

3. Bring the milk, cream and sugar almost to the boil, stirring constantly so that the sugar dissolves, it usually goes pretty fast. Then lift it from the heat and let it rest while you proceed.

4. Take four small serving bowls in baking pottery and a roasting pan. Boil water and pour up to half the edge of the pan.

5. Whisk the egg yolks fluffy and then add them to the warm vanilla and crème sauce while whipping it constantly. Pour it into the individual serving bowls and place them in the water bath.

6. Bake the crema catalana for about an hour until it has set and got some colour. Then take out the whole thing, lift out the cups from the water bath and let them cool. You can always prepare the dessert up to this point and then store them in the fridge.

7. Then, when it's time to serve the dessert, sprinkle a little white sugar in a thin layer on all the puddings and then put them for a while in the oven under the grill at maximum temperature.

8. Here you have to keep an eye on them since they colour quite quickly just before they are ready. Alternatively, if you have a gas burner, you can burn the sugar on top with that. The surface should be crispy.

CRISPY TOFFEE BISCUITS

Here you can fully use your own imagination, depending on whether you want to have several small, or a few larger biscuits. I like them a little larger but thin, but that's a matter of taste.

INGREDIENTS

75g butter

85 grams of sugar

40 grams of rolled oats

60 grams of flour

½ teaspoon vanilla powder

¼ teaspoon baking powder

2 tablespoons cream

2 tablespoons syrup

DO LIKE THIS

1. Melt the butter and mix the other ingredients straight into the pot and you'll save a little washing up.

2. Then spoon out the batter on to a baking tray, preferably lined with baking paper, since this will also save you washing up.

3. Bake at 200 degrees Celsius for approx 5-7 minutes until the biscuits have a golden brown colour. It's best to keep an eye on them as their colour tends to change quite quickly at the end. Then let them cool on a plate.

To drink? Well my suggestion is the Cava with that sherry like dosage that I mentioned earlier in the chapter. It is made by Freixenet and is called Malvasia. You can, of course, match the biscuits with a semi-sweet or sweet normal Cava or, if you like, even a dry Cava if you prefer to accentuate the sweetness in the dessert and the freshness in the Cava. It's all up to you.

CHOCOLATE CAKE WITH CANDIED ALMONDS AND HAZELNUTS

Dark chocolate and regular traditional Cavas can be a bit difficult to match in my opinion but there are some Cava styles that are perfect. One of my favourites I mentioned in the crema catalana recipe and that type of Cava also works well with this chocolate cake.

INGREDIENTS

3 eggs

380 grams of granulated sugar

5 tablespoons cocoa powder

1 teaspoon vanilla powder

½ teaspoon salt

150 grams melted butter

130 grams of flour

DO LIKE THIS

1. Preheat the oven to 175 degrees Celsius.

2. Beat eggs and sugar until its really fluffy. Add the melted butter, cocoa, vanilla and salt and whisk until smooth. Add the flour little by little.

3. Pour the batter into a buttered baking pan with a removable bottom, preferably also lined with breadcrumbs.

4. Bake in the middle of the oven for about 35 minutes but you need to check it, so it is not all runny in the middle.

5. Toast the almonds and hazelnuts in a hot frying pan. Reduce the heat and drizzle a little syrup and brown sugar over the nuts. Stir it quickly so that it all blends together and then put a spoonful on each plate together with the cake.

This cake almost tastes best the day after it's been baked so, if you're the planning type of person, you can bake it the day before and keep it ready in the refrigerator or in another cool place.

To drink? I would definitely serve a sweeter Cava with this cake since the sugar in the Cava will build a bridge to the bitterness of the chocolate cake, although I know that many would like to serve a rosé Cava together with chocolate. If so, I would suggest adding a raspberry sauce on the cake, then the aromas would match even better.

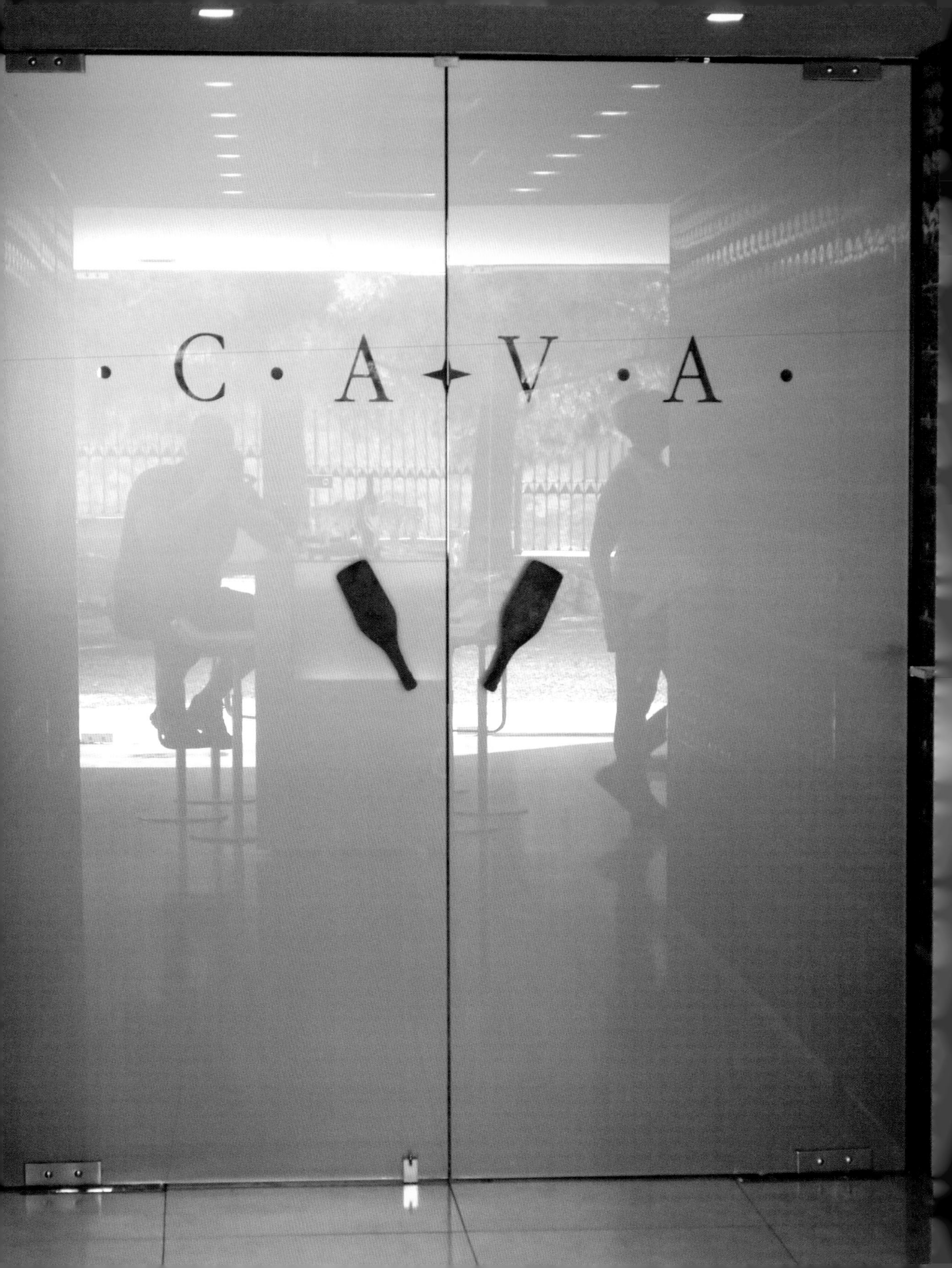
·C·A✦V·A·

WHAT EVERY CAVA FAN SHOULD HAVE IN STORAGE

I very rarely go to the wine shop and when I do, I never go on a Friday or Saturday. I would only do this if I was absolutely forced to and did not have any other choice. However, I do not think I will have to do this in the near future at least, since I live according to the Latin principle *"Praeparandus supervivet"*, "The one who is prepared will triumph"

Many people make a good habit of doing a weekly or monthly shopping when it comes to food, with cans of crushed tomatoes, minced beef to put in the freezer, pesto sauce, flour, eggs, milk and other things that might be good to have at home, so you are prepared and can cook a bit of everything. So do I, but I have also applied the same way of thinking to wine. I simply have everything at home in the basement. Oh, I don't mean that I have a wine cellar full of nice wines from Bordeaux slowly aging there - such extravagances can't be afforded. However, I do have wines that fill a good purpose, that are nice and affordable and that I know will keep for a while. That way, I know that no matter what we cook at the weekend when our friends come over, I won't need to rush to the wine shop on Friday after work. I have better things to do on a Friday than to queue with the rest of the Swedish population, whether it is at the wine shop or elsewhere.

Earlier I wrote that the prevalent view among Cava producers is that Cava is a perishable commodity, at least the more common varieties that we usually find when in the shops. This means that they should not be stored for any longer periods of time but it does not prevent you from having a few bottles in the cellar or in the refrigerator. If you gradually start to love Cava in the way that I have come to do, there is little risk that you will let the bottles get old, because you will keep track of when you bought them and see to invite your friends and loved ones to enjoy them in good time.

If you want to build a little stock of Cava at home, I recommend the following; do not buy several bottles of something before you know that you like it, even though someone else recommended it. You might not have the same tastes. Try your way through the brands and styles and when you find something you like, then you can take the opportunity to buy some and put it down in your cellar. In this way, you will naturally grow a little stock in your basement so that you will be ready for any celebration, when friends come over or you just feel like having a glass of Cava.

Since my friends have got used to Cava being served in one way or another when we have dinner at our house, I consider it my duty to have

a brut nature or brut ready in the fridge. You never know when you'll have friends over for a visit, or get invited to the fabulous neighbours for moules marinières. It can happen at any time!

During the summer months or when I'm in the mood, I prefer rosado, or rosé as we usually call it. Some of my absolute favourites are rosados, so there is always one in the fridge on a regular basis. Brut or brut nature, I always buy enough of, so I have some bottles in the basement that I can fill up the refrigerator with, if needed. I have developed the habit of having about three varieties at home at any time, a few bottles of each, so that I have something to choose from. Diversity is the spice of life and usually when I find something I like, I drink it for a while and then I find something else that becomes a favourite for a while. If my husband and our

friends like it too, the Cava in question usually stays on a bit longer. It comes naturally.

Apart from some younger (Reservas) brut and brut nature, that can be used for anything really, we also have some kind of Gran Reserva in our racks and usually some bottles of hundred percent xarel-lo Cavas. I'm not saying you need to store very many bottles of each style, but at least one bottle can be good to have. Take one that you have tested and that you know you like. I go down to get the Gran Reservas to put on ice when I need them, for example, when we fire up the barbecue and make grilled entrecote with a mild herb sauce and salad. However, there's no need to hurry to drink these Gran Reservas since their long slow aging down into the producer's cellars makes them capable of managing some time in your basement too.

Then we come to the beloved dessert Cavas. I think there are some that are fantastic and I have my favourite recipes that I serve them together with. Not everyone is fond of sweet stuff and if you are one of these people you can just choose to not drink them, but I find that when I serve Cava to a dessert, many people are very happily surprised, so it's probably worth taking a chance. Although I do not serve Cava each time I make a dessert, I do have at least two varieties in the cellar. One is a regular semi-seco that I can serve with sorbet and fruit, for example, and one a proper dulce, that I may have with creamy desserts.

With all these Cavas I stand ready for most kinds of dinners and guests. But as you might guess, I do not have just Cava in my basement but apply the same procedure to all other wines. Change and variation is a good thing.

Did you know that …

The vintages 1978, 1983, 2000, 2006, 2007, 2008, 2013 and 2016 are considered as exceptionally good vintages. So, if you see any of these take the opportunity to try one.

HAVE A TASTING AT HOME

To sit and taste wines at home is the foundation if one wants to develop ones' abilities for smell and taste. To try many different varieties, whether it is wine, beer or Cava, is the key to getting to know the differences and also to discover what styles you personally enjoy and appreciate. It is only when you start to think about it that you can seriously figure out why you prefer one wine to another.

But how is one to start? Well, you have to start at the beginning, because if you are an inexperienced taster you will often not be able to take in all the aromas and flavours in a complex beverage. The impressions are too many and the brain can only take in so much at once. Therefore, it might be an idea to start with the standard range, among the Cavas that are not so expensive. It is precisely here where the exciting journey begins and perhaps you also will, as I did, find some inexpensive favourites that will stay with you.

To get an idea and to start building up your smell and taste memory, or palate, as it is also called, the easiest way is to compare wines with each other. At first you can start by comparing two at a time, and then expand to four. Of course, you can try more than four at once but it is easy to get a bit numb in the nose if you are not used to it. I still rarely test more than four

at a time, because I simply think that if I have more I can't give the wines enough space and respect. Maybe it sounds silly, but that's me.

A practical tip is to taste wine with some friends, as it can be a bit too much to have up to four opened bottles of sparkling wine in the fridge after you're done. It would also be so sad if they stood there and went flat. Some Cavas are available in half bottles and they are a perfect size if you're only two people who want to sit at home and do some tasting.

The first step is obviously to buy what you want to try. My advice is that you start with the cheapest Cavas that you find on the shelf and then work your way up pricewise. Usually you will find more aromas in the pricier product you buy so by starting in the lower price range you will be able to keep track of the flavours that are being added as you go up in price. You will also realize how quickly the quality increases when you leave the really low-price stuff.

Once you have gathered your friends and put the Cavas on ice, you need to find glasses that suit. Ideally you want a tulip-shaped glass with a narrow base. Then the bubbles will be released from a limited area and they will stay longer in the glass. Also, the aromas will be kept in the glass so that

you get a chance to smell them before they disappear. It is here that the traditional Champagne flutes with straight sides fail. Their steep sides let all the aromas rise right out of the glass and you will not be able to smell half as much.

When you are to taste a wine, you should only fill your glass a little, maybe one third, in order to be able to gently swirl the glass and thus release more aromas. Swirl the glass - but then all the bubbles will disappear, you might think. Not to worry if you swirl it with a little caution, you do not need to spin it for king and country, or compete with your neighbour to see who can come closest to the brim without spilling.

Do you think it's hard to swirl the glass? In that case, you can put the glass on the table and "draw" a circle with the foot of the glass at just

the right speed and then you will get a good spin in the glass.

Now it's time to get to work and you are all sitting with filled glasses and a pen and paper ready. Your first meeting with the Cava is very important. "You never get a second chance to make a first impression", the saying goes, so give the Cavas you have before you in the glasses a fair chance. Agree with your friends that you take the first minutes to yourselves and stay quiet, until everyone has had time to smell and taste their way through the varieties. That way, all of you will have formed some kind of idea about the wines before you start to discuss and influence each other.

How do you go about it practically? Well, you always start with the glass on the far left. I personally think it is easiest to smell all the wines once before I begin to taste them, because this way I can quickly pick up the differences. But find a way that works for you. You can also smell and taste Cava number one, write down your impressions and then move on to the next one in line. The important thing is that you are focused as you spin the glass a little and smell the aromas, for that first impression is so special. Write down everything you recognize in terms of aromas and taste, even if you think it seems weird. I've had a tasting where one of the girls suddenly exclaimed, "Burnt hair! It's smells of burnt hair", after she had long pondered on what it was that she smelled so strongly, and many agreed with her I should add. The thing with fragrance and scent memories is that we all have our very own unique memories and no one can say that your sense of smell is wrong.

Through our childhood we are exposed to different scents and odours depending on the environment surrounding us, and we will connect certain smells to certain memories. Our upbringing also affects the smells we find easy to pick up and recognize, namely those we have been subjected to frequently and for long periods of time. Just think of the smell of the sea. I can almost promise you that anyone who grew up on the coast will have a much easier time recognizing the light sea tones in a wine than someone who grew up in woody inland areas where water was scarce. While someone brought up on the coast probably cannot relate as easily to the scents of pine forests.

So, if you think a wine smells of fireworks or burnt hair then it does and just because I can't smell the same, it doesn't mean you are wrong. So stand up for your own sense of smell!

When you have smelled and tasted your way through all the Cavas, I think you should open up and compare what you thought among yourselves. This is the whole reason why it's so good to try wines together. There will inevitably be times when someone is sitting there smelling or tasting something and in desperation will say "I smell it so clearly but I just can't find the word". Nothing is more frustrating! But if you're a few people there may be someone else who has smelled the same thing and actually found the definition.

The best thing is to discuss what you have come up with, because in my experience this is when people learn from each other. In addition, if you are a small group who meet and taste wine together

regularly, I promise that you will quickly find that you get better and better at expressing yourselves, in terms of aromas and flavours. However, it takes some time to get used to the smells and flavours that are typical for Cava, so be patient.

When you are done with comparing impressions and notes, it's always fun to see which of the Cavas that were the favourites. Here it is important that all of you have first figured out which one was your own personal favourite and also why you thought it was so good. Whenever my Cava group has a tasting they know that this question will come and then it is not enough just to say this or that wine. Oh no! No vote is taken if there is not an argument to back it up. For how are you going to recommend wines to friends and acquaintances in the future if you cannot tell them why you recommend it? That's only logical isn't it.

¡BARCELONA!

Barcelona is a wonderful city and perhaps the best weekend getaway in Europe in my opinion. Situated right by the Mediterranean with its beaches along the city line, the amazing architecture, the football fanatics, the never-ending pulse of Las Ramblas, the fantastic restaurants and bars, the harbour with its luxury yachts and with the surrounding green hills, Barcelona has it all.

To write a full guide to Barcelona could probably take a life-time, but I have some favourite places that I want to share with you, that I really think you should experience if you have the chance to visit "Barna", as the Catalans call the city for short.

Barcelona is a city full of wonderful architecture and old classical buildings with wide boulevards and narrow streets, so I suggest that you take a walk. There is nothing better than to walk the streets looking at the houses along the way from Plaza de Cataluña all the way down the Las Ramblas, taking a left down through the gothic parts and then along to the harbour and finally reaching the beach looking out over the Mediterranean.

If you only have a weekend I recommend you to walk to one or two of Gaudi's houses like

Casa Batlló or Casa Milà, also called "La Pedrera" and at least take a look at the outside. Of course, you just have to see the magnificent *Sagrada Familia*, the amazing cathedral that just takes your breath away. It is a true masterpiece inside and out.

But walking down the *Las Ramblas* with its high pulse is also something that you should not miss and half way down you can take a right turn into the covered market La Boqueria and stroll around looking at the fish, fruit, ham, candy and restaurants inside. If you get hungry, there is a fantastic little restaurant that is my absolute favourite, *El Quim*. Here you get wonderful tapas and Cava while you sit along a bar counter watching the guys working. Try the eggs with caramelized foie gras if they still have it on the menu, it is amazing.

The gothic old parts further down Las Ramblas and to the left are full of small shops and restaurants in the narrow streets that fill to the brim in the evening with hungry and thirsty people. Here you can find all kinds of food and drink, from Irish pubs to Cava bars. It is easy to get the feeling that you are lost, but don't worry it is a small area and you will soon come out on the other side. Last time we got lost in the old parts we found a fantastic little bar called *La Alcoba*

Azul where we stopped for a drink before dinner. And I must say that they made a fantastic sangria and also mojito, I really hope they will still be there next time I'll come by. So, it is not so bad to get lost after all.

If you continue towards the harbour you will come across another bar called *Can Paixano*, or if you ask for directions you can just ask for La Champangeria and people will know what you mean. You usually have to squeeze your way in since it is very small and terribly crowded. Here Cava is sold by the glass and you can also buy some snacks if you are hungry. Can Paixano is a favourite place among tourists, so you will hear many languages and probably run in to someone from your own country. I always do at least. But if it is good Cava rather than atmosphere you are looking for, this is not the place for you.

If you want instead to sit down at a restaurant and be sure to be served the best quality food, you should book a table or just show up at *Botafumeiro*. This is a very traditional and famous restaurant among the locals and definitely worth a visit. They are specialized in seafood and it seems that you can order anything here as long as it comes from the sea, no matter how strange. We went there after a recommendation from my friend Rafael who is himself from Barcelona and I can tell you that it was by far the best we ate during our stay. Now we go there every time we're in Barcelona.

There are of course many more places in Barcelona to visit but when it comes to food and drink there is always some new restaurant or bar opening and others closing. So I will leave you with these few recommendations that I

sincerely love and that have all been around for ever and ever. But while your there in Barcelona, take a chance and try to find your own favourites because there is so much to explore! [4]

Can Paixano
Carrer de la Reina Cristina, 7
www.canpaixano.com

Botafumeiro
Calle Gran de Gràcia 81
http://www.botafumeiro.es

---

[4] If you find something you really like, please send me an e-mail so I can go there too!

THE CAVA LADY

Since I first started doing research for the first edition of this book, I have also been writing a blog, and I still do. My nickname "The Cava Lady", which was something I got from a producer during my reasearch has stayed with me and become my brand. Now The Cava Lady is also the name on my website and it has followed me into social media, as in Facebook and Instagram. If you want more information, tips on good cavas to buy and try or just follow me and my family's travles through cava country you now know where to find me. And if you ever feel you want to come in contact with me, feel free in what ever way is most convenient for you. All my details are on the website.

www.thecavalady.com

Now I will bid you farewell and hope that you have learned something or at least been a bit inspired. Most of all I hope that you have a greater feeling about cava now than when you started reading this book.

I hope I'll see you in Penedès in the future!

Big hugs and cheers! May you live long and prosper!

/The Cava Lady

WORDS AND EXPRESSIONS IN SPANISH

Botellas en rima – bottles stacked horizontally

Bozal - steel halter

Brotación – Bud Burst

Brut – Cava with max 12 grams of sugar per litre

Brut Nature – Cava with no sugar added

Degüelle – disgorgement

Dulce – Cava with more than 50 grams of sugar per litre

El prensado – the pressing

El suelo – soil

Envero – Verasion/growth/maturation

En punta – on its head

Extra Brut – Cava with max 6 grams of sugar per litre

Extra seco – Cava with 12-20 grams of sugar per litre

Fermentación – fermentation

Gran Reserva – Cava aged at least 30 months

Injerto – grafting

La cupada – mix or blending

La poda – pruning

Licor de expedición – dosage

Removido – remuage

Reserva – Cava aged at least 15 months

Rosado – Rosé

Seco – Cava with 17-35 grams of sugar per litre

Semi Seco – Cava with 33-50 grams of sugar per litre

Tapón de expedición – crown-cap

Vendimia – Harvest

THE PRODUCERS

After my many travels in the region I must say that I have still not visited them all, but one day I will. Poco a poco as they tell me in Spanish, little by little.

When you decide to visit beautiful Penedès yourself, I suggest that you have a look at some of the producers that you might be ecpessially interested in. If you are interested in the bigger houses like Freixenet or Codorníu, you can just go there since they have visitors centers and are very much used to tourists. But if you want to visit some of the smaller producers, I suggest that you call or write them an e-mail in advance. You can ofcourse just pop in to see them, but there is always a risk that everyone is out working the vineyards.

The Catalans are warm hearted, welcoming and caring, and they will take the best care of you, I have no doubt!

AGR.I SEC.C.DE LLORENÇ DEL PENEDES, SCCL
Llorenç del Pdes
info@coopllorens.com

AGRICOLA ANOIA, S.L.
Piera
info@cavagabarro.com

AGRICOLA CASA SALA, S.A.
S.Quintí de Mediona
freixenet@freixenet.es

AGRICOLA DE BARBERA, SCCL
Barbera de la Conca
cobarbera@doconcadebarbera.com

AGRICOLA I SEC. DE CREDIT ESPLUGA, SCCL
L'Espluga de Francolí
coespluga@telefonica.net

AGRUPACIO VITICULTORS ARTESANALS, S.L.
S. Llorenç d'Hortons
marcmassana@maset.com

AGUSTI TORELLO, S.A.
S.Sadurní d'Anoia
info@agustitorellomata.com

ALBET I NOYA, S.L.
Subirats
albetinoya@albetinoya.com

ALTA ALELLA, S.L.
Tiana
celler@altaalella.cat

ANDRES VALIENTE E HIJOS, S.L.
Requena
info@vegalfaro.com

ANGLADA FERNANDEZ, Esteban
S. Sadurní d'Anoia

ANTONIO MASCARO, S.L.
Vilafranca del Pdes.
mascaro@mascaro.es

BATLLE Y MONTSERRAT, S.L.
Els Monjos
markelcava@terra.es

BENEIT MIR, Domingo
S.Sadurní d'Anoia

BERRAL I MIRO, S.L.
S.Sadurní d'Anoia
info@berralmiro.com

BODEGAS BILBAINAS, S.A.
Haro
j.barrero@bodegasbilbainas.com

BODEGAS BORDEJE, S.L.
Ainzón
pedidos@bodegasbordeje.com

BODEGAS CA N'ESTELLA, S.L.
S. Esteve Sesrovires
canestella@fincacanestella.com

BODEGAS CAPITA VIDAL, S.L.
El Pla del Pdes.
capitavidal@capitavidal.com

BODEGAS ESCUDERO, S.A.
Gravalos
bodega@bodegasescudero.com

BODEGAS FAUSTINO, S.L.
Oyón
info@bodegasfaustino.es

BODEGAS GRAN DUCAY, S.COOP.
Cariñena
bsv@bodegasanvalero.com

BODEGAS HISPANO SUIZAS, S.L.
Requena
info@bodegashispanosuizas.com

BODEGAS J. TRIAS, S.A.
Vilafranca del Pdes.
bodegas@jtrias.com

BODEGAS LANGA, HNOS., S.L.
Calatayud
info@bodegas-langa.com

BODEGAS MARCELINO DIAZ, S.A.
Almendralejo
bodega@mdiaz.com

BODEGAS MUGA, S.L.
Haro
info@bodegasmuga.es

BODEGAS MUR BARCELONA, S.L.
S.Sadurní dAnoia
info@mur-barcelona.com

BODEGAS ONDARRE, S.A
Viana
bodegasondarre@bodegasondarre.es

BODEGAS PEÑALBA LOPEZ, S.L.
Aranda de Duero
torremilanos@iconet.es

BODEGAS ROMALE, S.L.
Almendralejo
romale@romale.com

BODEGAS TROBAT, S.A.
Garriguella
toni.madern@bmark.es

BODEGAS Y VIÑEDOS ARTADI, S.A.
Laguardia
info@artadi.com

BODEGUES BERDIE ROMAGOSA, S.A.
Castellvi de la Marca
info@berdieromagosa.com

BODEGUES SUMARROCA, S.L.
Subirats
sumarroca@sumarroca.es

BONET CABESTANY, S.L.
S.Sadurní d'Anoia
info@bonetcabestany.com

BUTI MASANA, M. Blanca
S.Sadurní d'Anoia
butimasana@butimasana.com

C. FERRET, S.A.
Font-Rubí
ferret@cavasferret.com

CAL DAMIA, S.L.
S.Sadurní d'Anoia

CAL GASSET, S.L.
Solivella

CALAF VIDALES, Francesc
Nulles

CAN DESCREGUT, S.L.
Vilobí del Pdes.
candescregut@hotmail.com

CAN QUETU, S.L.
S.Sadurní d'Anoia

CAN RAFOLS DELS CAUS, S.L.
Avinyonet del Pdes.
canrafolsdelscaus@canrafolsdelscaus.com

CANALS CASANOVAS, Pedro
Subirats
info@canalscasanovas.com

CANALS NADAL, S.L.
El Pla del Pdes.
cava@canalsnadal.com

CANALS Y DOMINGO, S.L.
S.Sadurní d'Anoia
canalsydomingo@terra.es

CANALS Y MUNNE, S.L.
S.Sadurní d'Anoia
info@canalsimunne.com

CANO PEÑA, Leonardo
Vallbona d'Anoia
lcanop@eresmas.com

CARLES DE LAVERN, S.A.
Subirats
info@carlesdelavern.com

CASTELL D´AGE, S.A.
S. Llorenç d'Hortons
info@castelldage.com

CASTELLBLANCH, S.A.
S.Sadurní d'Anoia
castellblanch@castellblanch.es

CASTELO DE PEDREGOSA, S.L.
S.Sadurní d'Anoia
admin@castelodepedregosa.com

CAVAS DEL CASTILLO DE PERELADA, S.A.
Vilafranca del Pdes.
cavasvilafranca@castilloperelada.com

CAVAS HILL, S.A.
Olérdola
cavashill@cavashill.com

CAVAS LAVERNOYA, S.A.
Castellet i la Gornal
lavernoya@lavernoya.com

CAVAS PARES BALTA, S.A.
Pacs del Pdes.
paresbalta@paresbalta.com

CAYTUSA, S.L.
Ainzón
bodegascaytusa@hotmail.com

CELLER CAN BATLLE, S.C.P.
Avinyonet del Pdes.
info@artcava.com

CELLER CAN PUJOL, S.L.
Vilanova i la Geltrú
cellercanpujol@cellercanpujol.com

CELLER CARLES ANDREU, S.L.
Pira
info@cavandreu.com

CELLER COOP. I SEC. DE CREDIT VILA-RODONA, SCCL
Vila-Rodona
copvilar@retemail.es

CELLER COOPERATIU D' ARTES, SCCL
Artés
artium@cavesartium.com

CELLER J. MESTRE, S.L.
Tiana
disa.s.l.@teleline.es

CELLER JOSEP M.FERRET, S.L.
Font-Rubí
ferretguasch@ferretguasch.com

CELLER REVERTE, SCP S
alomó
enricreverte@terra.es

CELLER VELL, S.A.
S.Sadurní d'Anoia
info@cellervell.com

CELLERS ALSINA, S.L.
El Pla del Pdes.
alsina@alsinasarda.com

CELLERS CAMP DE TARRAGONA, S.L.
La Secuita

CELLERS CAN SURIOL DEL CASTELL, S.L.
Font-Rubí
cansuriol@suriol.com

CELLERS CAROL VALLES, S.L.
Subirats
info@cellerscarol.com

CELLERS DE L'ARBOÇ I SEC.CREDIT,SCCL
L'Arboç
caycra@caycra.com

CELLERS GRAU DORIA, S.L.
Canyelles

CELLERS PLANAS ALBAREDA, S.L.
Vilobí del Pdes.
planasalbareda@yahoo.es

CELLERS VIVES GAU, S.L.
Aiguamurcia
mas.basserola@sct.ictnet.es

CEPAGE, S.L.

CHOZAS CARRASCAL, S.L.
Requena
administracion@chozascarrascal.es

COCA SOLER, S.L.
Turis
info@castelldelssorells.com

CODORNIU, S.A.
S.Sadurní d'Anoia
codinfo@codorniu.es

COLET RIUS, Joan
S.Sadurní d'Anoia

COLL, S.C.P.
La Múnia -Castellví M.

COLLDEJUI, S.L.
S.Sadurní d'Anoia
cava@solaraventos.com

COLOMER BERNAT, Cristina
S.Sadurní d'Anoia
ccolomer@cavescolomer.com

COOP. VIT. I C.A. DE MONTBLANC, SCCL
Montblanc
cmontblanc@jet.es

COOPERATIVA AGRICOLA DE ROCAFORT DE QUERALT
Rocafort de Queralt
corocafort@do-conca.org

COVIDES, SCCL
S.Sadurní d'Anoia
administracio@covides.com

COVINOSA
Mollet de Perelada
vinicola@vinicoladelnordest.com

CRUZ GARCIA Y ZAPATA, SCP
El Masnou
restaurante@lescavesrekondo.com

CUM LAUDE, S.A.
S.Sadurní d'Anoia
cavacumlaude@terra.es

CUSCO I ESTEVE, S.L.
Avinyonet del Pdes.
cuscoberga@cuscoberga.com

CUSCOMAS, S.L.
Piera
caves@cuscoicomas.com

DOMINGUEZ CRUCES, Francisco
S.Sadurní d'Anoia
cavasyvinos@xamfra.com

DOMINIO DE LA VEGA, S.L.
Requenainfo@dominiodelavega.com

ELABORACION DE VINOS ESPECIALES, S.L.
S.Sadurní d'Anoia

ENRIC NADAL, S.L.
Torrelavit
nadal@nadal.com

ESMEL, S.C.P.
S.Sadurní d'Anoia
cavaesmel@telefonica.net

ESPUMOSOS DE CAVA, S.A.
S.Sadurní d'Anoia
blancher@blancher.es

ESTEVE NADAL, Juan
Avinyonet del Pdes.
avinyo@avinyo.com

EXP. SADURNI BEGAS, S.A.
Begues
info@montaudesadurni.com

EXPLOT.VITIV.DEL PDES., S.A.
Torrelles de Foix

FABRE QUERALTO, Remei
S.Martí Sarroca

FELIX MASSANA, S.L.
S. Pau d'Ordal
felix@cavafelixmassana.com

FERMI BOHIGAS, S.A.
Odena
administracio@bohigas.es

FERRÉ I CATASÚS, S.L.
La Granada
info@castelldelmirall.com

FERRER MATA, S.L.
Subirats
info@elmasferrer.com

FINCA CASTELL DE SUBIRATS, S.A.
Subirats
rolivesa@terra.es

FINCA VALLDOSERA, S.A.
Olérdola
general@fincavalldosera.com

FONPINET, S.L.
S.Sadurní d'Anoia
cava@fonpinet.com

FONT VERDIELL, Josep
S.Sadurní d'Anoia

FORNS CARTRO, M. Rosa
Santa Fe del Pdes.
cava@fornsraventos.com

FREIXA RIGAU, S.A.
Capmany
comercial@grupooliveda.com

FREIXENET, S.A.
S.Sadurní d'Anoia
freixenet@freixenet.es

GASTON COTY, S.A.
S.Sadurní d'Anoia
lorigan@lorigancava.com

GENIS RICART, S.L.
Castellvi de la Marca

GERMANS BUNDO, SCP
Pacs del Pdes.

GIBERT ARISSA, Jaume
Artés
cavagibert@cavagibert.com

GIRO DEL GORNER, S.L.
Puigdàlber
gorner@girodelgorner.com

GIRO RIBOT, S.A.
Santa Fe del Pdes.
giroribot@giroribot.es

GONZALEZ BYASS, S.A.
S.Sadurní d'Anoia
vilarnau@vilarnau.es

GRAMONA, S.A.
S.Sadurní d'Anoia
cava@gramona.com

GRIMAU DE PUJADES, S.A.
Castellví de la Marca
vendes@grimau.com

HERETAT CAL RUBIO, SCP
Els Monjos

HERETAT GUILERA, S.L.
Subirats
info@cavaguilera.com

HERETAT MARINA, SCP
Font-Rubí

HERETAT MAS TINELL, S.L.
Vilafranca del Pdes.
info@mastinell.com

HERETAT MESTRES, S.L.
S.Sadurní d'Anoia
cava@mestres.es

HILDEMAR, S.A.
Olérdola

HUGUET DE CAN FEIXES, S.L.
Cabrera d'Anoia
canfeixes@canfeixes.com

INVIOSA
Almendralejo
info@lardebarros.com

J. B.BERGER, S.A.
Santa Fe del Pdes.
info@martiserda.com

J. GARCIA CARRION, S.A.
Vilanova i la Geltrú
jamell@jgc.es

J. M. RAVENTOS BLANC, S.A.
S.Sadurní d'Anoia
raventos@raventos.com

J. PUJADO, S.L.
Subirats

JANE BAQUES, S.L.
El Pla del Pdes.
janebaques@telefonica.es

JANÉ GARRIGA, Ramon
Avinyonet del Pdes.
mascandi@telefonica.net

JANE SANTACANA, S.L.
Santa Fe del Pdes.
janesantacana@janesantacana.com

JANE VENTURA, S.A.
El Vendrell
janeventura@janeventura.com

JAUME GIRO I GIRO, S.L.
S.Sadurní d'Anoia
cavagiro@cavagiro.com

JOAN RAVENTOS ROSELL, S.L.
Masquefa
bpons@raventosrosell.com

JOAN SARDÀ, S.A.
Castellví de la Marca
joansarda@joansarda.com

JOSEP MASACHS, S.L.
Torrelles de Foix
adm@cavasmasachs.com

JOSEP TUTUSAUS ANDRES, S.L.
Pontons
xamos@xamos.net

JOVE MARTI, Domingo
S.Martí Sarroca

JULIA BERNET, SCP
El Pago-Subirats
info@juliabernet.com

JUVE Y CAMPS, S.A.
S.Sadurní d'Anoia
juveycamps@juveycamps.com

LA XARMADA, SCCL
Pacs del Pdes.
laxarmada@laxarmada.com

LLAGRIMA D'OR, S.L.U.
S.Sadurní d'Anoia
llagrimador@ya.com

LLEURE OLESA, S.L.
Olesa de Bonesvalls
info@cavestutusaus.com

LLOPART ALEMANY, Jaume
Font-Rubí
info@jaumellopartalemany.com

LLOPART VILAROS, Pere
S.Sadurní d'Anoia
llopart@llopart.es

LLUCH LLUCH, Jordi
S.Quintí de Mediona
vinyaescude@vinyaescude.com

LUDENS, S.A.
Font-Rubí

MAINEGRA, S.A.
Mendavia
mainegrasa@terra.es

MARIA CASANOVAS I ROIG, S.L.
S.Sadurní d'Anoia
mariacasanovas@brutnature.com

MARIA OLIVER PORTI, S.L.
S.Sadurní d'Anoia

MARQUES DE MONISTROL, S.A.
S.Sadurní d'Anoia
aolive@haciendas-espana.com

MARQUES RIGOL, S.L.
Torrelavit
MARRUGAT, S.A.
Vilafranca del Pdes.
pinord@pinord.es

MARTI I SENDRA GERMANS, S.L.
Montferri

MAS ROMANI, S.A.
Font-Rubí
info@masromani.com

MASIA CAN MAYOL, S.L.
Vilobí del Pdes.
canmayol@interceller.com

MASIA CODINA, S.L.
Puigdálber
cavesmascodina@hotmail.com

MASIA EL MAS, S.A.
La Granada

MASIA GINEBREDA, S.L.
Sant Sadurní d'Anoia
masiaginebreda@hotmail.com

MASIA PUIGMOLTO, S.A.
Castellet i la Gornal
avalles@emendis.es

MASIA ROMAGOSA, S.L.
S.Martí Sarroca
cava@romagosatorne.com

MASIA VALLFORMOSA, SLU
Vilobí del Pdes.
vallformosa@vallformosa.es

MASOLIVE, S.A.
S.Sadurní d'Anoia
cavamasolive@yahoo.es

MASSANA NOYA, Eudald
Subirats
bodega@massananoya.com

MATA I COLOMA, S.L.
S.Sadurní d'Anoia
info@matacoloma.com

MEDALL ESTRUCH, Maria
Torrelavit

MIR VIDAL, Jaume
S.Sadurní d'Anoia

MOLINER CAMPS, S.L.
Sant Sadurní d'Anoia
cava@molinercamps.com

MONT MARÇAL VINICOLA, S.A.
Castellví de la Marca
mont-marcal@mont-marcal.com

MONTSERRAT ESTEVE, Pedro
S.Sadurní d'Anoia
cavas@condedevalicourt.com

MUNGUST, S.L.
Piera
cavesmungust@ya.com

OLERDOLAVINS, S.L.
Olérdola
torres@masrabassa.com

OLIVELLA BERTRAN, S.L.
Font-Rubí

OLIVELLA I BONET, S.A.
L'Arboç

OLIVELLA ROVIRA, Pere
Font-Rubí

ORIOL ROSSELL, S.A.
Castellet i la Gornal
oriolrossell@oriolrossell.com

PAGES ENTRENA, S.A.
Piera
cava@pagesentrena.com

PAGO DE THARSYS, S.L.
Requena
pagodetharsys@pagodetharsys.com

PARATO VINICOLA, S.L.
El Pla del Pdes.
info@parato.es

PARXET, S.A.
Tiana
parxet@parxet.es

PERE CANALS, S.L.
S.Sadurní d'Anoia
cava@castellsantantoni.com

PERE RIUS, S.L.
Castellví de la Marca
info@cavapererius.com

PERE VENTURA I FAMILIA, S.L.
S.Sadurní d'Anoia
info@pereventura.com

PEREZ ROURA, Juan A.
Alella
roura@roura.es

PICHER BODEGAS, S.L.
Sant Sadurní d'Anoia
info@cavapicher.com

PIJOAN ESCOFET, SAT
La Bisbal del Pdes.

PIÑOL TORRENTS, Joan
El Pla del Pdes.

POCH URPI, Nuria
S.Sadurní d'Anoia

PONS I FONT ELABORADORS, S.L.
La Granada
miquelpons@cavamiquelpons.com

PUIG MUNTS, S.L.
Martorell
puigmunts@puigmunts.com

PUJOL VILALLONGA, Juan
Cornellà de Ll.

RAMON CANALS CANALS, S.A.
Castellví de Rosanes
cava@canalscanals.com

RAVENTOS GUASCH, SCP
S.Sadurní d'Anoia
cava@raventossoler.com

RECAREDO MATA CASANOVAS, S.A.
S.Sadurní d'Anoia
cava@recaredo.es

RENE BARBIER, S.A.U.
S. Cugat Sesgarrigues
renebarbier@renebarbier.es

RESERVA MONT-FERRANT, S.A.
Blanes
montferrant@montferrant.com

REXACH BAQUES, S.A.
Font-Rubí
info@rexachbaques.com

RICARD M. DE SIMON, S.A.
S.Sadurní d'Anoia
nestfly@hotmail.com

RIGOL ORDI, M. Isabel
S.Sadurní d'Anoia

RIUDABELLA, S.A.
Vimbodi
info@riudabella.com

ROGER GOULART, S.A.
S.Esteve Sesrovires
rogergoulart@rogergoulart.com

ROS MASANA, Fèlix
S.Sadurní d'Anoia
rosmas@rosmas.com

ROSA Ma. TORRES, S.L.
Sarral
info@rosamariatorres.com

ROSELL JUANHUIX, Miquel
S.Sadurní d'Anoia

ROSELL MIR, Josep Mª
Subirats
josep@rosellmir.com

ROSELL Y FORMOSA, S.A.
S.Sadurní d'Anoia
rformosa@roselliformosa.com

ROSÉS VILA, Carles
Castellví de la Marca

ROVELLATS, S.A.
S.Marti Sarroca
rovellats@cavasrovellats.com

S.A.T. MAS LLUET Nº907
Castellví de la Marca
cavasbolet@cavasbolet.com

SABATE I COCA, S.A.
Subirats
info@castellroig.com

SADEVE, S.A.
Torrelavit
naveran@naveran.com

SADURNI COMAS CODORNIU, S.L.
S.Sadurní d'Anoia
scomasc@scomasc.com

SANCHO TORNE, Teresa
S.Sadurní d'Anoia
barralo@telefonica.net

SARDA TORRENTS, Pilar
S.Sadurní d'Anoia
almirallcava@yahoo.es

SEBIRAN, S.L.
Requena -Campo Arcís
bodegasebiran@bodegasebiran.com

SEGURA PUJADAS, Joan
Torrelavit

SEGURA VIUDAS, S.A.
Torrelavit
seguraviudas@seguraviudas.es

SIMO DE PALAU, S.L.
L'Espluga de Francolí
caves@simodepalau.com

SOLER DEGOLLADA, S.A.
Font-Rubí
info@cavamartinsoler.com

SOLER JOVE, S.A.
S.Sadurní d'Anoia
solerjove@sct.ictnet.es

TARRIDA I SIBIL, S.L.
Font-Rubí

TARRIDA LLOPART, Jordi
Font-Rubí

TORELLO LLOPART, S.A.
Gelida
torello@torello.es

TORNE CALDU, Fèlix
S.Sadurní d'Anoia
tornebel@gmail.com

TORRALLARDONA HNOS., SCP
S.Sadurní d'Anoia
caves@torrallardona.com

TORRE ORIA, S.L.
Requena
info.torreoria@torreoria.es

TORREDANOIA, S.L.
Piera
bonsol@bonsol.es

TORRENS MOLINER, S.L.
Piera
comercial@torrensmoliner.com

TORRES PRUNERA, S.L.
Vilafranca del Pdes.
info@torresprunera.com

TORRES SIBILL, Josep
S.Sadurní d'Anoia
cavabertha@cavabertha.com

U MES U FAN TRES, S.L.
Font-Rubí
umesu@umesufan3.com

UNION VINICOLA DEL ESTE, S.L.
Requena
j.hidalgo@uveste.es

V.C. MONASTELL, S.L.
S.Sadurní d'Anoia
ferrangironees@terra.es

VENTURA SOLER, S.L.
Subirats
info@venturasoler.com

VENTURA VENDRELL, Xavier
Subirats

VIA DE LA PLATA, S.L.
Almendralejo
cava@bodegasviadelaplata.com

VIADER CAYON, S.L.
S.Sadurní d'Anoia

VIDAL GARCIA, Mercè
Torrelavit

VIDAL MORGADES, Ramon
Aiguamurcia

VILADELLOPS VINICOLA, S.L.
Olérdola
viladellops@viladellops.com

VILAMAJO SAUMELL, Antoni
S.Sadurní d'Anoia
cava@vilamajo.com

VINICOLA DE SARRAL I SEC. DE CREDIT, SCCL
Sarral
cavaportell@covisal.es

VINICOLA I SEC.CREDIT S.ISIDRE DE NULLES, SCCL
Nulles
gerencia@vinicoladenulles.com

VINS EL CEP, S.L.
S.Sadurní d'Anoia
info@elcep.com

VIÑA TORREBLANCA, S.L.
Olérdola
info@vinatorreblanca.com

VIVES AMBROS, S.L.
Montferri
vivesambros@tinet.org

MY WARMEST THANKS!

The idea to this book came to me during a Cava tasting, during my sommelier studies, held by Mischa Billing, a famous wine personality in Sweden. Although Mischa was not aware at the time that the seed she had unknowingly planted in my mind would later grow into a book, I owe her my warmest thanks. Without her I might never have got the idea to actually embark on this journey.

Neither without my husband Andréas's help would I have made it all the way or even started. But with his commitment and support at home and during our travels, it all became possible and without his pictures the book would have been very dull indeed.

I also want to give my warmest thanks to Maria Del Mar Torres at Institut del Cava, and Rosó Gabarró Llombart (formally at Institut del Cava and now at Cavas Torelló) who has helped me with everything from visits to the producers, to answering my many questions and checking the manuscript over and over. Their interest and involvement all through my project really spurred me on and lit up my day when it's been a little tough. Also, Elisabeth Puyoles at Consejo Regulador del Cava has been a tremendous help, providing me with statistics and regulations.

The producers August Torello Mata, Codorniu, Freixenet, Gramona, Juve y Camps, Mont Marçal, Recaredo, Parés Baltà, Pere Ventura, Segura Viudas and Vilarnau, will always have a special place in my heart after opening their arms and welcoming me and Andréas with such warmth during their busiest time of the year, the harvest, when I was doing research for the first edition. I owe you lots of thanks! Big hugs also go to Veronica and Florian at Visit Penedès, where we have found a second home when we are in Penedès.

Last but not least I want to thank my publisher who wanted to update and print a second edition of the book and Graham Tucker, for checking my very colloquial language for the most obvious mistakes. Let's hope that we will reach many new Cava fans around the world!

A book does not write itself, nor would this one have been done without the help from all of these people and I am forever grateful for the support you have given me during this time! To old and new friends who have been involved I raise my glass and say;

¡Salud! Y Muchas Gracias!

SOURCES OF INFORMATION

Books

El Cava – Jordi Olavarrieta

Oenology – Josep Bujan & Jesús Artajona

The cellar, storing and caring for wine – Josep Bujan & Jesús Artajona

Viticulture – Josep Bujan & Jesús Artajona

Websites

Consejo regulador del Cava: www.crCava.es

Institut del Cava: www.institutdelCava.com

Freixenet: www.freixenet.es and www.freixenet.se

Codorniu: www.codorniu.com